SSR Paper 22

Leaving No One Behind, Leaving No One Unaccountable

Ombuds Institutions, Good (Security Sector) Governance and Sustainable Development Goal 16

Luka Glušac

DCAF Geneva Centre for Security Sector Governance

]u[
ubiquity press
London

Published by
Ubiquity Press Ltd.
Unit 3N, 6 Osborn Street
London E1 6TD
www.ubiquitypress.com

DCAF – Geneva Centre for Security Sector Governance
Maison de la Paix, Chemin Eugène-Rigot 2E, P.O. Box 1360
CH-1211 Geneva 1, Switzerland
www.dcaf.ch

First published 2023

Cover photograph: ©Parlamentsdirektion/Thomas Topf Cover photograph description:
Dr. Ramya Sundararaman, Deputy Director of the Defense Suicide Prevention Office
within the U.S. Office of the Secretary of Defense, addresses participants of the
15th International Conference of Ombuds Institutions for the Armed Forces (ICOAF),
hosted at the Austrian Parliament from 18–20 June 2023.

Print and digital versions typeset by Siliconchips Services Ltd.

ISBN (Paperback): 978-1-914481-36-9
ISBN (PDF): 978-1-914481-37-6
ISBN (EPUB): 978-1-914481-38-3
ISBN (Mobi): 978-1-914481-39-0

Series: SSR Papers
ISSN (Print): 2571-9289
ISSN (Online): 2571-9297

DOI: https://doi.org/10.5334/bcw

The full text of this book has been peer-reviewed to ensure high academic standards.
For full review policies, see https://www.ubiquitypress.com/

Suggested citation:
Glušac, L. 2023. *Leaving No One Behind, Leaving No One Unaccountable:*
Ombuds Institutions, Good (Security Sector) Governance
and Sustainable Development Goal 16. London: Ubiquity Press.
DOI: https://doi.org/10.5334/bcw. License: CC BY-NC 4.0

To read the free, open access version of this book
online, visit https://doi.org/10.5334/bcw or scan
this QR code with your mobile device;

Table of Contents

List of Tables and Figures

Tables

Figures

Dedication

To my parents, Slavko (1950–2015) and Magdolna, for their unconditional love and support.

About SSR Papers

The DCAF SSR Papers provide original, innovative, and provocative analysis on the challenges of security sector governance and reform. Combining theoretical insight with detailed empirically driven explorations of state-of-the-art themes, SSR Papers bridge conceptual and pragmatic concerns. Authored, edited, and peer reviewed by SSR experts, the series provides a unique platform for in-depth discussion of a governance-driven reform agenda, addressing the overlapping interests of researchers, policy-makers, and practitioners in the fields of development, peace, and security.

DCAF – Geneva Centre for Security Sector Governance is dedicated to improving the security of states and their people within a framework of democratic governance, the rule of law, respect for human rights, and gender equality. Since its founding in 2000, DCAF has contributed to making peace and development more sustainable by assisting partner states, and international actors supporting these states, to improve the governance of their security sector through inclusive and participatory reforms. It creates innovative knowledge products, promotes norms and good practices, provides legal and policy advice, and supports capacity-building of both state and non-state security sector stakeholders.

About the Author

Luka Glušac, PhD, is Research Fellow at the Institute for Philosophy and Social Theory, University of Belgrade. Before joining the Institute, he worked as Programme Manager at DCAF, Senior Adviser for the Ombudsman of Serbia, and National Institutions Fellow at the Office of the UN High Commissioner for Human Rights. Since 2019, he has sat on the Executive Board of the Belgrade Centre for Security Policy. His recent research and policy advice focuses on the institutional design of so-called fourth branch institutions, particularly ombuds institutions and anti-corruption agencies, as well as their relationship with domestic and international actors. He is particularly interested in their role in security sector governance. His training is in Political Science (PhD), International Security (MA), and Security Studies (BA) at the University of Belgrade. His articles have appeared in *Human Rights Law Review, Journal of Human Rights Practice, Netherlands Quarterly of Human Rights*, and *International Journal of Human Rights*, among others.
ORCID: https://orcid.org/0000-0002-7597-6839

Declaration

Acknowledgements

Although writing a book can be considered a lonesome endeavor, I wouldn't have done it without the support of many people. I would like to particularly thank:

Gabriela Manea, Alexandra Preperier, Alice Alunni, Richard Steyne, William McDermott, and anonymous peer reviewers for giving me such constructive and helpful feedback on my manuscript.

The participants for International Conference for Ombuds Institutions for the Armed Forces (ICOAF), for being an epistemic community that leads such thought-provoking and inspiring discussions.

Hans Born, for his friendship, and leadership during my time at DCAF, as well as for the insightful discussions we continue to have.

Daniel Reimers and Ajla Kuduzovic for being such a great team and keeping me in the ICOAF family.

Saša Janković, without whom I would probably never have become interested in ombuds institutions. Many ideas in this book have emerged from our discussions.

My colleagues at the Institute for Philosophy and Social Theory, University of Belgrade, for keeping listening to my ombuds stories, even though they are not always sure what I am jabbering about, and for creating the most enjoyable and stimulating work habitat.

Daliborka Nikodimović for her enduring friendship and never missing a chance to call me – she knows how.

'Puleni' (Peki, Duki, Srki, Keni) for being so invested in all the stages of the writing process, and keeping me well hydrated.

Sanja for love and support, and for creating the perfect environment which kept me motivated and centered in the critical stage of writing, during my retreat and her 'vacation' in Mali Lošinj.

My family (mom Magdolna and sisters Nada and Jelena), who I can never thank enough, for always being there for me, and keeping on being my stronghold.

Executive Summary

This study explores how ombuds institutions, here defined as independent oversight bodies that receive complaints and investigate matters pertaining to the protection and promotion of human rights and/or maladministration, can contribute to the realization of the 2030 Agenda on Sustainable Development and its Sustainable Development Goals (SDGs). The focus of the study is on SDG 16, because it is devoted to promoting peaceful and inclusive societies for sustainable development, providing access to justice for all, and building effective, accountable, and inclusive institutions at all levels. In other words, this SDG is aligned the most with the mandate and functions of ombuds institutions. Another reason for the focus on SDG 16 is the attempt of this study to add the security sector into the equation, where and when possible. This is done by connecting the SDG framework with the concept of security sector governance (SSG) and security sector reform (SSR), and the principles that guide them.

With their unique position in-between three branches of power, the mandate to oversee public administration (including the security sector) and protect human rights, ombuds institutions are well-placed to play an important role in national efforts to fulfil the SDGs. However, the key argument of this research is that their main role should be to support and contribute, not to lead. Achieving the SDGs calls for a strong web of institutions and partnerships. Ombuds institutions (and other forms of national human rights institutions: NHRIs) are central national human rights actors but must not be expected to lead the realization of human rights-based SDGs. They cannot be the only game in town. In fact, for a number of the SDG 16 targets, ombuds institutions should primarily serve as accountability mechanisms. They should work with, pressure, and make public administration accountable, in cases when the administration as the primary duty-bearer fails to protect the rights of citizens and when their actions fall short of the standards needed to achieve the SDGs. This particularly applies to security sector institutions, considering that their actions, particularly of the police and security services, may interfere with human rights in an unparalleled way, as they are authorized to use special measures to penetrate deep into the private lives of citizens.

The central assumption of this study is that ombuds institutions can contribute to achieving all SDG 16 targets. To demonstrate how this could be done in practice, the research explores the role of ombuds institutions in achieving SDG 16 by looking at both implementation and accountability. The former is captured under the title 'leaving no one behind' and the latter under 'leaving no one unaccountable.' Leaving no one behind is a central *credo* of the 2030 Agenda. It is highly relevant for SDG 16, as well as SSG/R, due to the centrality of the principles of responsiveness and participation, which posit that the security sector should respond to the security needs of all, and conversely, all should be involved, to the extent possible, in the development of security policies.

SDG 16 stresses the need for strong institutions that are built on respect for human rights, effective rule of law, and good governance at all levels. It is arguably one of the most ambitious goals in the 2030 Agenda because it is not simply a goal by itself but also an enabler for the achievement of other goals. Nonetheless, as this study demonstrates, many SDG 16 targets are rather vague, and limited guidance exists on how to measure and achieve them, especially in fragile contexts. This study thus provides guidance and recommendations to ombuds institutions and other actors on how to best support each other in achieving SDG 16.

CHAPTER I

Introduction

In 2015, the United Nations Sustainable Development Summit adopted the 2030 Agenda for Sustainable Development – a plan of action for people, planet, and prosperity, that seeks to strengthen universal peace in larger freedom and eradicate poverty in all its forms and dimensions, as stated in the opening sentences of its preamble. To achieve this, the summit formulated 17 Sustainable Development Goals (SDGs).

The SDGs were an attempt to revolutionize the understanding of development, to create a framework that was more fit for purpose to tackle the daunting challenges a global society faces. It is becoming increasingly evident that the world is rapidly breaching the capacity of earth systems to support life and facing growing inequalities at all levels (Caballero 2019: 138).

The governments that have signed onto the 2030 Agenda certainly exude confidence about the impending positive impact of their 'historic decision' (2030 Agenda 2015: 6), especially in relation to realizing human rights. The commitment to human rights is expressed already in the preamble and is then reinforced by several assurances to the effect that the new text is 'grounded in' the Universal Declaration of Human Rights, in international human rights treaties, and 'other instruments such as the Declaration on the Right to Development' (2030 Agenda 2015, 8). Historically, human rights and development have had two different trajectories, rarely communicating clearly and systematically with each other. Such a commitment to human rights in the 2030 Agenda was very welcome. It has also meant that human rights actors and mechanisms must be closely engaged in the realization of the 17 SDGs.

Like their predecessors (Millennium Development Goals – MDGs), the SDGs are a statement of aspirations: a voluntary agreement rather than a binding treaty (Pogge & Sengupta 2016: 1). While this presents a drawback insofar as states may be more tempted to skirt their commitments, it also presents an opportunity insofar as states may be willing to adopt a more ambitious agenda when this agenda imposes on them no legally binding obligations (Pogge & Sengupta 2016: 1). Indeed,

How to cite this book chapter:
Glušac, L. 2023. *Leaving No One Behind, Leaving No One Unaccountable: Ombuds Institutions, Good (Security Sector) Governance and Sustainable Development Goal 16*. Pp. 1–4. London: Ubiquity Press. DOI: https://doi.org/10.5334/bcw.a. License: CC BY-NC 4.0

the 2030 Agenda comes with a great promise – to eradicate poverty and hunger, to strengthen universal peace in larger freedom, and to protect the human rights of all.

The 2030 Agenda has established the High-level Political Forum on Sustainable Development (HLPF) as the central United Nations platform for the follow-up and review of the Agenda and the SDGs. While being needed and valued as a global reporting and coordination forum, HLPF has a modest influence vis-à-vis the implementation of the SDGs. The global goals are meant to be implemented on the national level by the national authorities. With states' history of successful elusion from even strong legal obligations, many observers have rightly been worried about how they would approach the fulfilment of a voluntary pledge.

In view of this challenge, recent academic research – and to a greater extent, grey policy literature – has started to address the related questions 'Through what processes can SDG accountability be assured at the national level?', 'By which standards can SDG action be assessed?', and 'With what effect can governments be held to account for their SDG-related commitments?' (Karlsson-Vinkhuyzen, Dahl & Persson 2018). This emerging literature has identified parliaments and independent oversight agencies, such as ombuds institutions and other forms of national human rights institutions (NHRIs), as essential cornerstones for national SDG accountability regimes (Breuer & Leininger 2021: 5). However, these studies have not gone far enough in explaining how ombuds institutions and other forms of NHRIs could and should contribute to achieving the SDGs (particularly given the strong emphasis on human rights in the 2030 Agenda) and making governments accountable. This research aims to help fill in this literature gap, by concentrating on SDG 16. The focus is on this particular goal, because it is devoted to promoting peaceful and inclusive societies for sustainable development, providing access to justice for all, and building effective, accountable, and inclusive institutions at all levels. In other words, it is aligned the most with the mandate and functions of ombuds institutions.

Another reason for the focus on SDG 16 is the attempt of this study to add the security sector into the equation, when and where possible. This will be done by connecting the SDG framework with the concept of security sector governance (SSG) and security sector reform (SSR), and the principles that guide them.

SSG includes both 'the formal and informal influences of all the structures, institutions and actors involved in the provision, management and oversight of security and justice at national and local levels' (Myrttinen 2019: 13). SSR, as defined by the UN (UN DPKO 2012: 2), is a process of assessment, review, and implementation as well as monitoring and evaluation led by national authorities that has as its goal the enhancement of effective and accountable security for the State and its peoples without discrimination and with full respect for human rights and the rule of law.

SSG is the application of these principles of good governance to security provision in a particular national setting (DCAF 2015). Looking at the conceptual relationship between SSG and SSR, following Myrrtinen (2019: 14), good SSG could be regarded as 'the goal,' whereas 'SSR, or security sector transformation, is a way of getting there.' If there are problems with the administration of SSG in a particular country in a way that its security sector 'is not inclusive, is partial and corrupt, unresponsive, incoherent, ineffective and inefficient and/or unaccountable to the public' (Schnabel 2012: 53), that country's security sector is in need of reform (Dursun-Özkanca 2021: 12).

SSR can be described as a road to achieving good SSG, which shares the goal of having effective, accountable, and inclusive institutions with SDG 16. Such a goal applies to both security providers and security overseers. As ombuds institutions are understood as important elements of the security sector oversight system (DCAF 2019; IPU & DCAF, 2003: 89; United Nations 2012: 98), this research seeks to provide additional insights on how this nexus between SSG and SDG 16 plays out in practice.

The central assumption of this study is that ombuds institutions can contribute to achieving all SDG 16 targets. With their unique position in-between three branches of power, with the mandate to oversee public administration (including the security sector) and protect human rights, ombuds institutions are well-placed to play an important role in national efforts to fulfil the SDGs.

However, the key argument of this research is that their main role should be to support and contribute, not to lead. Achieving the SDGs calls for a strong web of institutions and partnerships. Ombuds institutions (and other forms of national human rights institutions; NHRIs) are central national human rights actors but must not be expected to lead the realization of human rights-based SDGs. They cannot be the only game in town, because they cannot secure effective remedies for citizens who claim that their rights have been violated on their own (Glušac 2018b: 62). Successful partnerships are crucial, as NHRIs can be neither a panacea for all human rights-related problems nor a replacement for other mechanisms of control and protection (Glušac 2017: 67). Their *raison d'être* can only be fulfilled in synergy with other functional stakeholders (Glušac 2017: 67).

Some governments downplay, ignore, or violate human rights. In such contexts, ombuds institutions could be inspired to step in and take the lead, trying to compensate the lack or negative consequences of government actions. While this can bring some short-term success, in long run it is not sustainable. Ombuds institutions cannot achieve human rights-focused SDGs on their own. They should push the government to perform. The same applies to their role in security sector oversight. Ombuds institutions and other types of NHRIs should be there to advise their governments, correct their actions, and advance both legislation and practice. To demonstrate how this could be done in practice, the research explores the role of ombuds institutions in achieving SDG 16 by looking at both implementation and accountability. The former is captured under the title of 'leaving no one behind' and the latter under 'leaving no one unaccountable'.

Leaving no one behind is a central *credo* of the 2030 Agenda. It is highly relevant for SDG 16, as well as SSG/R, due to the centrality of the principles of responsiveness and participation, which posit that the security sector should respond to the security needs of all, and conversely, all should be involved, to the extent possible, in the development of security policies.

Where do people face disadvantages due to ineffective, unjust, unaccountable, or unresponsive national authorities? Who is affected by inequitable, inadequate, or unjust laws, policies, processes, or budgets? Who is less able or unable to gain influence or participate meaningfully in the decisions that impact them? These questions are at the very heart of SDG 16, which stresses the need for strong institutions that are built on respect for human rights, effective rule of law, and good governance at all levels. It is arguably one of the most ambitious goals in the 2030 Agenda because it is not simply a goal by itself but also an enabler for the achievement of other goals. Nonetheless, as it will be seen, many SDG 16 targets are rather vague, and limited guidance exists on how to measure and achieve them, especially in fragile contexts. To that end, this study aims to provide some additional guidance to ombuds institutions and other actors.

As Robert Putnam (1993: 63) notes, 'Who governs?' and 'How well?' are the two most basic questions of political science. Translated to the language of the 2030 Agenda, one could ask 'Who implements?' and 'How well?' A negative response to the second question brings the issue of accountability into the picture. As already alluded to, the issue of accountability is highly relevant for the implementation of the SDGs. This study attests that for a number of the SDG 16 targets, ombuds institutions should primarily serve as accountability mechanisms. They should work with, pressure, and make public administration accountable, in cases when the administration as the primary duty-bearer fails to protect the rights of citizens and when their actions fall short of the standards needed to achieve the SDGs. This particularly applies to security sector institutions, considering their actions, particularly of the police and security services, may interfere with human rights in an unparalleled way, as they are authorized to use special measures to penetrate deep into the private lives of citizens (Glušac 2018b).

There is an additional reason why ombuds institutions are so relevant for the SDGs. They contribute to making the entire endeavor more locally owned. Local ownership is a central concept for both SSR and development. The concept has its roots in the development circles that empha-sized the importance of empowering local communities and encouraging local participation, while at the same time it is widely regarded as the bedrock and main precondition for successful SSR (Gordon 2014). Being national state authorities with rich experience in applying international standards to the national (local) context, ombuds institutions could serve as a social fibre of the SSR and SDG efforts. In the right environment, they could help build trust among international, national, and local actors, liaising between them when frictions occur, and making sure that all social forces are included in the process, and that their needs and interests are duly considered.

Before presenting the road map of the study, one note on terminology. This book is about ombuds institutions. Still, not all ombuds institutions contain the term 'ombuds' or 'ombudsman' in their official title, despite their common structural and functional characteristics. For instance, in Francophone Africa, many countries have ombuds institutions but formally call them '*mediateur*,' while Botswana and South Africa use the term 'Public Protector.' The majority of other African states use the term 'ombudsman.' Similarly, ombuds institutions in Europe have different names, e.g., People's Advocate (Albania), Parliamentary Advocate (Moldavia), Public Defender of Rights (Czechia), Defender of People (Spain), Justice Provider (Portugal), Chancellor of Justice (Estonia, Finland), Commissioner for Human Rights (Russia, Azerbaijan), Human Rights Defender (Armenia), etc. These different designations do not imply substantial differentiation but usually emanate from the traditions of the particular legal terminology of a state. A good example of this variety of names is the official translation of the European Ombudsman, the ombuds institution of the European Union: Médiateur européen (French); Defensor del Pueblo Europeo (Spanish); Provedor de Justiça Europeu (Portuguese); Mediatore europeo (Italian) (Glušac 2019c: 5).

The term 'ombudsman' is gender-neutral, as the 'man' suffix itself is gender-neutral in origi-nal Swedish. That is, it applies correctly whether the ombudsman is male or female. However, many states expressly provide a notation for female incumbents ('Ombudswoman,' 'Ombudsfrau,' 'Médiatrice'). To avoid ambiguity and overcomplicated language, this research uses the gender-free term 'ombuds institutions' throughout. It uses 'ombudsperson' when referring to an indi-vidual mandate-holder. Such a decision also reaffirms the function-centered approach to ombuds institutions taken by in this research.

The study is organized as follows. It starts with defining ombuds institutions, their key features, mandate, and functions (Chapter 2). This chapter then elaborates on the concepts of good govern-ance and good security sector governance, with a focus on the principles of good (security sector) governance, before connecting good governance with security, human rights, and development. The study then turns to explaining the nature of ombuds institutions as security sector and devel-opment actors, before presenting the original methodological framework for analyzing their role in achieving SDG 16 (Chapter 3). In the next two chapters, this framework is applied empirically. They start with providing more details on the logic and background of 'leaving no one behind' (Chapter 4) and 'leaving no one unaccountable' (Chapter 5), respectively, before going target by target, demonstrating the potential role of ombuds institutions in achieving them. The concluding chapter (6) provides an overview of the study and its main findings and brings a set of recommen-dations to different actors on how to support ombuds institutions.

CHAPTER 2

Setting the Scene

Ombuds institutions: definition, mandate, and functions

Evolution, definition, and mandate

Traditionally, ombuds institutions have been understood as public-sector institutions, preferably established by the legislative branch of the government to assess, as a rule, the administrative activities of the executive branch (Reif 2004: 1). The International Bar Association has similarly defined the ombuds institution as an office provided by the constitution or by the action of the legislature (parliament) and headed by an independent high-level public official, who receives complaints from aggrieved persons against government agencies, officials, and employers, or who acts on his or her own motion, and has the power to investigate, recommend corrective actions, and issue reports (Ferris, Goodman & Mayer 1980: 2). This administrative focus of ombuds institutions reflects their origins.

The first-ever (in today's terms) ombuds institution was established in Sweden in 1809 as a parliamentary representative, with the task to safeguard the rights of citizens by establishing a supervisory agency that was completely independent of the executive. This Swedish model is usually called the classical administrative ombuds or first-generation ombuds institution. It was to remain the only one for a long time. In 1919, Finland adopted the ombuds idea in a republican constitution for the first time. Nevertheless, it was Denmark that initiated its increasing popularity and, by creating a new legal structure in the mid-1950s, became a role model for its further development. This Danish model is sometimes referred to as a second-generation ombuds institution, as it has abandoned the strict Swedish legal approach and introduced a less formal complaint procedure. In 1963 this legal structure was adopted by Norway, in 1967 by the United Kingdom, and later by the Netherlands. These institutions have thus been focused on maladministration. The European

How to cite this book chapter:
Glušac, L. 2023. *Leaving No One Behind, Leaving No One Unaccountable: Ombuds Institutions, Good (Security Sector) Governance and Sustainable Development Goal 16*. Pp. 5–24. London: Ubiquity Press. DOI: https://doi.org/10.5334/bcw.b. License: CC BY-NC 4.0

Ombudsman (1997:23) has defined maladministration as that which 'occurs when a public body fails to act in accordance with a rule or principle which is binding upon it.'

The collapse of authoritarian regimes in Portugal, Spain, and Greece, as well as Central and Eastern Europe and the resulting process of democratization, provided new incentives for the idea of the ombuds institution. Portugal and Spain have introduced so-called third-generation ombuds – hybrid or human rights ombuds institutions – as their ombuds institutions were given an explicit mandate to protect and promote human rights, in addition to fighting maladministration. With that, ombuds institutions have been inaugurated as human rights mechanisms, which has changed their approach, provided them with the opportunity to address systemic issues, and extended their reach. By combining the basic concepts of both the rule of law and human rights, hybrid ombuds institutions have lifted the entire ombuds concept to a new level. Consequently, ombuds institutions have been made attractive for countries across the world. Hybrid ombuds institutions today represent a most frequent model in Europe and Latin America.

Africa has an interesting mix of models. The first ombuds institution in Africa was established in Tanzania in 1966, followed by a few more ombuds institutions through to the 1980s. However, the popularity of the ombuds and other national human rights institutions considerably increased in Africa only in the 1990s.

To sum up, the two most recognizable ombuds models are administrative and hybrid (which includes the human rights function). The latter can fulfil the criteria necessary for the status of a national human rights institution (NHRI). NHRIs are independent state-funded statutory bodies mandated to protect and promote human rights on the national level. The establishment and operations of an NHRI must conform to the Paris Principles on NHRIs, as adopted by the UN General Assembly's Resolution 48/134 in 1993. Despite being legally non-binding, the Paris Principles have great political weight. They are the main international reference providing the basic principles and characteristics of an NHRI. The Paris Principles set forth a number of conditions that an institution has to fulfil in order to be recognized and accredited as an NHRI, including establishment under primary law or the Constitution, a broad mandate to promote and protect human rights, formal and functional independence, pluralism (representing all aspects of society), adequate resources and financial autonomy, freedom to address any human rights issue arising, annual reporting on the national human rights situation, and cooperation with national and international actors, including civil society (UNGA 1993).

The accreditation is conducted by the Subcommittee on Accreditation (SCA) of the Global Alliance of NHRIs (GANHRI), whose accreditation system is recognized and facilitated by the UN. To be able to conduct accreditations in consistent and procedurally fair manner, SCA has adopted the General Observations on the Paris Principles, which serves as its authoritative interpretation.

The institutions which are awarded with the highest accreditation – A – can participate fully in sessions of the UN Human Rights Council and take the floor under any agenda item, submit documentation, and take up seating, separate from the state delegation. They can also interact directly with the UN treaty bodies and the Universal Periodic Review, including through the submission of their independent parallel reports, and participation in their sessions and follow-up activities.

As of April 2023, a total of 88 institutions worldwide fulfils the Paris Principles and are thus accredited as A-status NHRIs (GANHRI n.d.). Around 35% of them are (hybrid) ombuds institutions, mostly from Europe and Latin America. Other accredited institutions come in the form of human rights commissions, and to a much lesser degree, human rights institutes.

Some countries have opted to have both a general ombuds institution and human rights commission (or similar collective body). In Europe, this is the case in Scandinavian countries, Ireland, and the Netherlands, while in Africa, such a set-up exists in, for instance, Burkina Faso, Chad, Côte d'Ivoire, Mali, Nigeria, Tunisia, and Uganda. Some ombuds institutions are multi-member bodies. Ghana has incorporated its classical ombuds institution into the new multi-member Commission on Human Rights and Administrative Justice, while Tanzania did the same in 2000 when it created the

Commission for Human Rights and Good Governance, which absorbed the oldest ombuds institution on the continent. Similarly, the National Human Rights Institution of Finland consists of the Parliamentary Ombudsman and the Human Rights Centre along with its Human Rights Delegation.

Although in the past, there was a considerable difference between ombuds institutions and human rights commissions, such a distinction has almost ceased to exist with the emergence of hybrid ombuds institutions and the development of contemporary national human rights institutions. The accreditation in line with the Paris Principles has been a decisive factor in this process (Glušac 2021: 51–52).

Two related notes are necessary here. First, the Paris Principles define individual complaint-handling as an additional function of NHRIs, not a compulsory one. For ombuds institutions, complaint-handling is an essential (primary) function. Second, traditionally ombuds institutions had been designed as *ad personam* institutions, meaning that an ombudsperson was a high public official who was the institution him/herself, where the office was established to help that individual in fulfilling the mandate. In other words, it was a single-headed institution, contrary to the human rights commission as a collective or collegiate body. However, as the gap between the two models started to shrink, this delineation also blurred. Some countries have introduced ombuds institutions as collegiate bodies, as in Bosnia and Herzegovina (Institution of Human Rights Ombudsman of Bosnia and Herzegovina) and Austria (The Ombudsman Board), or collective bodies, with the chairperson being appointed among the members, as in Kenya with the Commission for Administrative Justice (Office of the Ombudsman). Although this difference between single-headed or collective body does not (necessarily) imply differences in mandate or functions, it does influence internal organization and responsibilities.

Finally, the ombuds concept has witnessed an expansion both vertically and horizontally. Some countries have established ombuds institutions on national, regional, and local levels (such as Serbia), while others have a well-developed network of regional and local ombuds institutions but without the national ombuds office (such as Italy). Ombuds institutions have also been established through and for various sectors, creating the difference between general (parliamentary) and specialized ombuds institutions. Hence, specialized ombuds institutions have been established for universities, consumers' rights, tax, patients' rights, police, or armed forces.

Considering its aim and focus, this research concentrates on general (parliamentary) ombuds institutions, as well as those ombuds institutions specialized in the security sector (police or armed forces). The latter include, for instance, the institutions such as the German Parliamentary Commissioner for the Armed Forces, the Parliamentary Ombud's Committee for the Norwegian Armed Forces, or the South African Military Ombud.

Given this increased diversity among ombuds models and shrinking conceptual distance between ombuds institutions and other forms of national human rights institutions, this research covers all these institutions under the label 'ombuds institutions,' as long as they fulfil the following criteria:

- they are independent institutions, appointed by the Parliament, or by the joint decision of the legislature and the executive;
- they are mandated to handle individual complaints;
- they operate on the national level;
- they have the right to advise the government on the human rights/administrative policy and, ideally, on legislation.

In other words, for the purpose of this research, ombuds institutions are defined as independent oversight bodies that receive complaints and investigate matters pertaining to the protection and promotion of human rights and/or maladministration.

This research uses the term 'ombuds institutions' throughout. The term 'national human rights institutions' (NHRIs) is used only when referring to a specific document or event explicitly mentioning 'NHRIs.'

Independence

Ombuds institutions are, by rule, appointed and supervised by the parliament to which they report. In fact, in a number of countries (e.g., Hungary, Lithuania, Ukraine, Finland), the term 'Parliamentary' is even explicitly included in the official title of the national ombuds institution to make this institutional connection as clear as possible (Glušac 2019a: 534). However, as an ombuds institution is an independent oversight authority, the parliament must not interfere with the work of this body or issue specific instructions and orders to it. The same applies to the executive, irrespective of the fact whether it participates in the appointment of the ombudsperson or not. In some countries, particularly in Africa and Asia, the executive branch has an important role in appointing the ombudsperson. Ideally, the ombudsperson should never be appointed upon the sole decision of the executive. More complex appointment procedures which include both the executive and parliament are much more suitable, while appointment by parliament is preferred option, as it guarantees the highest degree of independence.

Independence presupposes that ombuds institutions should be free from the influence of any political authority. As reaffirmed by former Serbian Ombudsperson Saša Janković, ombuds' independence is not 'a privilege established for anyone's comfort, but a requirement and a necessity needed to ensure that human rights protection does not depend on daily politics' (OHCHR 2012).

Independence is a key characteristic of the ombuds institution (Langtry and Roberts Lyer 2021). It is its *conditio sine qua non*; without independence, an ombuds institution stops being an ombuds institution (Glušac 2021: 45). The independence means that ombuds institutions' decisions are not influenced by any external entity. This applies not only to parliament and the executive, but also to the other branches of the state, and any other public or private entity, such as companies, civil society organizations, and citizens, including complainants. If the ombuds institution is established by the constitution, then the independence is most usually constitutionally guaranteed; otherwise, it is granted by the legislation (founding law).

The literature recognizes different aspects and types of independence of oversight and regulatory bodies (Born & Buckland 2011; Hanretty & Koop 2013). This research differentiates four essential aspects of independence: institutional, functional (operational), personal, and financial. Institutional means that an ombuds institution is independent of the government and, more specifically, that it is not part of any of the bodies that it is mandated to oversee. Whilst institutional independence relates to the position of the office vis-à-vis other institutions, functional (operational) refers to the office's ability to decide which matters and priorities to pursue, free from interference by other institutions or actors (Born & Buckland 2011: 11). Personal independence relates to the security of the ombudsperson's position and tenure in office, including a legally established tenure of office, clear procedures for the potential removal of an ombudsperson from office, and a narrowly defined set of criteria stipulating the circumstances under which this can happen (Born & Buckland 2011: 10). Finally, financial independence means that an ombuds institution obtains and manages its funds independently from any of the institutions over which it has jurisdiction (Born & Buckland 2011: 9). In other words, ideally, the ombuds institution should draft, and the Parliament should adopt, its budget. The Venice Principles on the Ombudsman (Venice Commission 2019: para. 21) particularly highlight financial independence:

> Sufficient and independent budgetary resources shall be secured to the Ombudsman institution. The law shall provide that the budgetary allocation of funds to the Ombudsman institution must be adequate to the need to ensure full, independent and effective discharge of its responsibilities and functions. The Ombudsman shall be consulted and shall be asked to present a draft budget for the coming financial year. The adopted budget for the institution shall not be reduced during the financial year unless the reduction generally applies to other State institutions. The independent financial audit of the Ombudsman's budget shall

take into account only the legality of financial proceedings and not the choice of priorities in the execution of the mandate.

These four aspects of independence are mutually dependent. Absence of any of these robs the institution of independence. All four aspects of independence must be guaranteed by the law. However, such a normative (de jure) foundation of independence is just a basis for actual or de facto independence (see more in Lacatus and Carraro 2023).

Ombuds institutions are de jure (formal) independent to the degree to which the legislation forbids any external influence on their work, in terms of the offering of instructions, inducements, threats, or consideration of political or other preferences. De facto (actual) independence refers to the degree to which the agency takes day-to-day decisions without any external interference coming from political parties, authorities they oversee, the media, or the citizens. Ombuds institutions must take their decisions without taking into consideration any explicit or implicit, expressed or intended, wishes or interests of external entities.

With their unique position, independent of three traditional branches of government, ombuds institutions are a kind of auxiliary component to the checks and balances between state powers. Thus, they have increasingly been described as part of the fourth branch of government, together with other independent constitutional (expert) oversight bodies.

Functions

The Venice Principles on the Protection and Promotion of the Ombudsman, the most elaborated set of principles related to ombuds institutions, adopted by the Council of Europe in 2019, stipulate that 'the mandate of the Ombudsman shall cover the prevention and correction of maladministration, and the protection and promotion of human rights and fundamental freedoms' (Venice Commission 2019: para. 12). Another key international standard applicable for ombuds institutions, the Paris Principles on national human rights institutions, while specifying that those institutions should be mandated to protect and promote human rights, clarify that the human rights mandate should be interpreted in a broad, liberal, and purposive manner to promote a progressive definition of human rights which includes all rights set out in international, regional, and domestic instruments, including economic, social, and cultural rights (GANHRI SCA 2018).

Neither Venice nor Paris Principles define 'protection' and 'promotion' of human rights. However, the SCA of the GANHRI, the expert peer body in charge of accreditation, do provide useful guidelines in this regard. The SCA understands 'promotion' to include those functions which seek to create a society where human rights are more broadly understood and respected. Such functions may include education, training, advising, public outreach, and advocacy. 'Protection' functions may be understood as those that address and seek to prevent actual human rights violations. Such functions include monitoring, inquiring, investigating, and reporting on human rights violations, and may include individual complaint handling (GANHRI SCA 2018). The main weakness of this classification is that it neglects the so-called normative or legislative function, which is explicitly captured in some other conceptualizations of ombuds functions. For instance, Castro differentiates between the protective, preventive, and normative functions of ombuds institutions (Castro 2019: 66).

In Castro's classification, the protective function relates to safeguarding citizens' rights and interests, exercised through handling complaints with a view to securing redress of grievances. The protective function also includes the right of the ombuds institution to lodge individual appeals for relief against rights infringements, such as *habeas corpus* and *recurso de amparo* (Spanish Ombudsman and Peruvian Ombudsman) (Castro 2019: 67).

The preventive function is oriented to influencing the policy level in order to improve the quality of government and public service delivery, by recommending legislative or regulatory reforms, or changes to institutional practices. In such cases, the institution plays what Jacoby calls the 'role of reformer' (Jacoby 1999: 34). The preventive function is performed through own-initiative investigations (the Dutch Ombudsman and Peruvian Ombudsman) or the preparation of special reports (UK Ombudsman and Peruvian Ombudsman), which allow the ombuds institution to focus on general problems and to recommend changes in the administration (Castro 2019: 67). In this classification of ombuds functions, educational activities fall within the preventive function. As argued by Jacoby, when the recommendations arising from the ombuds' investigations are aimed at ensuring that the administration does not make similar mistakes in the future, the institution effectively exercises the educational function (Jacoby 1999: 37). The same function is performed when the institution provides trainings to citizens, civil society organizations, or interest groups about its role, and their rights as citizens; or to civil servants to identify shortcomings in government organization and contribute to improving service quality (Castro 2019: 68).

The third main function attributed to the ombuds institution in this differentiation is its normative function or authoritative function in the development of legal norms (Castro 2019: 68). As noted by Addink (2019b: 6), the ombuds institution as a fourth-power institution develops and applies legal norms, which are an important feature of administrative functioning regarding the protection of citizens as well as supervision of administrative behavior. The institution's contribution to the production of legal norms hinges on the authoritative character of the ombuds' opinion (Castro 2019: 84).

This study adopts the division between the protection and promotion functions, as understood by the SCA, with one important note. The normative function is subsumed under the protection function because its purpose is to advance legislation, enhance the level of human rights protection, and prevent human rights violations. To that end, it falls under the protection functions, as envisaged by the SCA, as it contributes to the efforts to 'address and … prevent actual human rights violations.' Such a normative sub-function is different from 'advising' which is part of the promotion function. This research takes 'advising' as those types of ombuds institutions' advice addressed to public authorities (including government and parliament) that do not require legislative changes. In other words, 'advising' falls under 'promotion,' whilst 'legislative or normative advice' constitutes part of 'protection.'

The following sub-functions in Table 1 can be recognized within these two main ombuds functions:

Table 1: Main functions of ombuds institutions (by author)

Main functions	Protection	Promotion	Additional functions (examples)
Subfunctions	monitoring	education	Fighting corruption
	inquiring	training and research	National Preventive Mechanism against Torture, under UN OPCAT
	investigating (upon complaint or own-motion)	advising	Independent Monitoring Mechanism (IMM), under UN CRPD
	reporting	public outreach and advocacy	
	mediation		
	litigation		
	legislative advice		

Monitoring

Monitoring is an umbrella term describing various activities ombuds institutions use to collect, verify, and use the information to address human rights problems in the country. Monitoring is a process of systematically tracking the activities of and actions by a government with the ultimate objective to reinforce the state's responsibility to respect, protect, and fulfil human rights. To that end, it has a temporal quality in that it generally takes place over a protracted period of time (OHCHR 2001: 9).

Monitoring is performed in order to ascertain whether a state respects its human rights obligations, rooted in both international human rights law and national laws and regulations. The ultimate purpose of monitoring is to improve the human rights situation. This can be done through different sets of activities: by establishing a record of what has taken and/or is taking place; by intervening with the authorities to force the government to answer for or remedy the situation; by informing higher levels of the organization or making the general public aware of human rights violations to prompt wider political reactions. The exact way in which the monitoring is carried out, and what is monitored, will depend on the situation in the country at the time (Mæhlum 2008).

Monitoring is thus an overarching approach that ombuds institutions use to keep track of their countries' human rights records. All ombuds institutions' activities should ultimately contribute to an increased ability of the institution to assess the human rights situation in the country, on individual and systemic levels.

Investigation and inquiry

Ombuds institutions shall have discretionary power, on their own initiative or as a result of a complaint, to investigate cases related to maladministration or human rights violations. The standards of ombuds investigation derived from the Venice and Paris Principles include:

- the right to request the cooperation of any individuals or organizations who may be able to assist in its investigations;
- the right to unrestricted access to all relevant documents, databases, and materials, including those which might otherwise be legally privileged or confidential; this includes the right to unhindered access to government buildings;
- unhindered and unannounced access to prisons and any other institutions where persons may be detained, or their rights restricted;
- the power to interview or demand written explanations of public officials, civil servants, and authorities.

The right to investigate should extend to all alleged human rights violations, including the military, police, and security officers (GANHRI SCA 2018).

The administrative authorities subject to the ombuds´ investigation should be bound to the duty of cooperation. This implies that the administration must facilitate the supervisory activities of the ombuds institution by providing information and access to government buildings, and employees.

Some authors and national legislations recognize the difference between investigation and inquiry in the ombuds context. However, there is no single criterion that could help generalize such a distinction. For instance, Castro uses the term 'inquiry' to refer 'specifically to those investigations conducted by the ombudsman to address the complaints lodged by the citizens', compared to own-initiative investigations (Castro 2019: 61). Some institutions use this distinction for a different purpose. Some NHRIs in the form of human rights commissions use inquiries for egregious or systematic human rights issues (that they typically initiate themselves), while instead almost all human rights ombuds institutions use own-motion investigations for the same purpose. For instance, the Human Rights Commission of the Maldives uses 'investigation' for individual cases, while 'inquiry' relates to systemic or thematic investigations. The study adopts this approach.

The most frequent output of investigations is recommendation. All ombuds institutions are vested with the authority to give recommendations to public authorities. Depending on jurisdictions, recommendations may come as single acts or as part of the report. They usually come in the form of a separate act when ombuds institutions determine there was a human rights violation or another omission (wrongdoing) in an individual case. In those cases, the 'recommendation' is an individual written act consisting of an overview of the complaint, the main findings of the ombuds' investigation, and a recommendation (or recommendations) with justification. The recommendation may also come as part of the report resulting from a systemic (or thematic) investigation. In other jurisdictions, as in the Netherlands or the United Kingdom, ombuds recommendations always come together with the report, whether it is a result of an individual or systemic investigation.

A recommendation means a specific proposal by the ombuds institution on how the wrongdoing should be remedied (if it is an individual case), or how legislation or administrative regulations or practices should be changed (if it is a systemic report with recommendations). The ombuds institution focuses on the procedural aspects of the administrative structure, but it is not precluded from examining the substance of the law regulations that may have led to maladministration in a particular case (Castro 2019: 62). Thus, after an objective investigation, the recommendation of the ombuds institution may include suggested amendments to government policy or practice, and even legislation (Castro 2019: 62).

The ombuds' recommendations are *stricto sensu* not legally binding, having a soft-law character. The impact of recommendations is not derived from binding, coercive, or determinative powers of ombuds institutions, but from the rigor, objectivity, and independence with which they conduct their investigations (Glušac 2020: 7). Because the institution has no power of enforcement, ombuds institutions rely on persuasion and publicity as a means to 'force' the compliance with its recommendations. Although the administrative bodies to which the recommendations are addressed are not obliged to implement them, their formal feedback is required. They are obliged to report back to the ombuds institution, to state if they have implemented the recommendation(s), and if not, to explain why. The Venice Principles (2019: para. 17) stipulate that ombuds institutions 'shall have the legally enforceable right to demand that officials and authorities respond within a reasonable time set by the ombuds institution.'

Reporting

All ombuds institutions produce reports. Together with recommendations, reports are the most visible outputs of the work of ombuds institutions. All ombuds reports serve to highlight key human rights developments in a country and provide a public account, and therefore public scrutiny, of the effectiveness of an ombuds institution. As argued by the SCA, the reports also provide a means to make recommendations to the government and monitor respect for human rights by the government (GANHRI SCA 2018).

The reports of ombuds institutions can be national or international; as well as annual, special (thematic), or case reports. International reports refer to submissions to international human rights mechanisms, such as UN treaty bodies or Council of Europe's monitoring bodies. The duty and the right to submit reports to the parliament and international human rights mechanisms are enshrined in all relevant international standards, including the Paris, Venice, and Belgrade Principles.

As ombuds institutions are most usually appointed by parliament, they report to the legislature as well. They are required to submit an annual report on their activities to the parliament. This reporting fulfils several functions, as noted by Castro (2019: 63):

> First of all, the ombudsman accounts for its activities. Second, the annual report can render grievances transparent to the parliament and enable it to employ its own competencies within the democratic control of the administration. In this respect, the ombudsman functions as an auxiliary body of the parliament. A third important function of reporting is the imposition of a form of soft sanction in case of non-compliance with recommendations. Finally, the reporting activity of the ombudsman can draw the attention of parliament to the necessity for amendments to legislation.

In addition to annual reports, ombuds institutions are usually empowered to submit special (thematic) reports. These reports cover a particular topic, by providing an in-depth analysis of a concrete human rights or (mal)administration issue, and often include general recommendations aimed at improving the quality of the government by proposing changes in institutional practices, procedures, or regulations (Castro 2019: 63).

Many ombuds institutions regularly report to universal and regional human rights mechanisms. This function is particularly underlined in the Paris Principles, which recognize engaging with the international human rights system, in particular the Human Rights Council and its mechanisms (Special Procedures and Universal Periodic Review) and the United Nations Human Rights Treaty Bodies, as an effective tool for the promotion and protection of human rights domestically (see Glušac 2022).

Mediation

In addition to the right to initiate and conduct investigations, and to address recommendations, ombuds institutions often have the right to conduct mediation and offer good services. This is, for instance, provided explicitly in the Law on the Protector of Citizens (Ombudsman) of Serbia (2021: Art. 27):

> In addition to the right to initiate and conduct investigations, the Protector of Citizens shall have the right to act preventively by providing good services, mediation and giving advice and opinions on issues within his/her sphere of competence, with a view to improving the work of administrative bodies and protection of human rights and freedoms.

Indeed, for some authors, the resolution of disputes is an integral part of the protective function of the ombuds institution (Remac 2014: 5). Not only does the institution protect citizens against the administration, but it also solves disputes between citizens and the administration, for example in cases when the conduct of the administration was not strictly illegal or irregular, but damage was done to the citizen.

While both are well recognized methods of dispute resolution and are often used interchangeably, there is a difference between good services and mediation. In the case of good services, the ombuds institution serves to bring two sides to the table, but does not actively participate in the process once that happens. When it comes to mediation, the ombuds institution actively works with two parties on finding a solution to the problem (conflict), including by suggesting possible solutions. Such an engagement of ombuds institutions should always be voluntary and should not seek to undermine or interfere with the duty to investigate allegations of human rights violations, where that duty applies (McGregor, Murray & Shipman 2019: 338).

It should be mentioned that human rights commissions, and especially equality bodies, use mediation to settle individual complaints more much often than ombuds institutions. A form of mediation more frequently used by ombuds institutions is the mediation of broader social conflicts. For instance, the Peruvian ombuds institution (*Defensoría del Pueblo*) often performs an important role as a mediator in social conflicts, helping to reduce costs for both the individual and the administration (Castro 2019:67). Ombuds institutions of Costa Rica and Kenya are also known for their mediating efforts. In mediating between the parties, the ombuds institutions must always retain their independence and impartiality (Remac 2014: 6).

(Legislative) advice

As mentioned above, this study recognizes two types of advising: policy and legislative. The former relates primarily to human rights and administrative policy, and how to improve the policy and its implementation. The latter refers to the so-called normative function of ombuds institutions and deserves more attention here.

Most general ombuds institutions are explicitly empowered to submit parliamentary bills (Kucsko-Stadlmayer 2008: 50–51). The Paris Principles also authorize NHRIs to recommend either the adoption of new or the amendment of existing legislation or administrative arrangements (OHCHR 2010: 105). The Belgrade Principles, a key international reference document on relations between NHRIs and parliaments introduced in 2012, endorsed by the UN (UNGA 2012: para. 67), have identified five principles pertaining to the legislative relations between NHRIs and parliaments: (1) NHRIs should be consulted by parliaments on the content and applicability of a proposed new law with respect to ensuring human rights norms and principles are reflected therein; (2) parliaments should involve NHRIs in the legislative processes, including by inviting them to give evidence and advice about the human rights compatibility of proposed laws and policies; (3) NHRIs should make proposals of amendments to legislation where necessary, in order to harmonize domestic legislation with both national and international human rights standards; (4) NHRIs should work with parliaments to promote human rights by legislating to implement human rights obligations, recommendations of treaty bodies, and human rights judgments of courts; and (5) NHRIs should work with parliaments to develop effective human rights impact assessment processes for proposed laws and policies (Belgrade Principles 2012: para. 27–31).

The Venice Principles also stipulate that in the framework of the monitoring of the implementation at the national level of ratified international instruments relating to human rights and fundamental freedoms and of the harmonization of national legislation with these instruments, ombuds institutions shall have the power to present, in public, recommendations to parliament or the executive, including to amend legislation or to adopt new legislation. The legislative role of ombuds institutions is also expressed through encouraging ratification of, or accession to, international human rights instruments, and the effective implementation of international human rights instruments. The Paris Principles prescribe that NHRIs should promote and encourage the harmonization of national legislation, regulations, and practices with these instruments (GANHRI SCA 2018).

Ombuds institutions may also have an active role in performing an *ex-post* evaluation of legislation or post-legislative scrutiny (PLS), understood as a broad form of review, the purpose of which is to address the effects of the legislation in terms of whether the intended policy objectives have been met by the legislation and, if so, how effectively (UK Law Commission 2006: 7). Studies have demonstrated that ombuds institutions and other NHRIs have already been conducting activities most relevant for PLS, even though those have not been often labelled as such, neither formally by parliaments nor by scholarly literature (Glušac 2019d: 155). In other words, their de facto role in PLS has already been well established through their practice, despite the often-lacking de jure recognition by parliamentary procedures (Glušac 2019d: 155).

Finally, many ombuds institutions have the power to initiate proceedings before the Constitutional Court for the assessment of the constitutionality and legality of laws, other regulations, and general acts. This is explicitly stipulated in the Venice Principles, providing for ombuds institutions' power to challenge the constitutionality of laws and regulations or general administrative acts (Venice Commission 2019).

Additional functions

Besides their core mandate and functions presented above, ombuds institutions often receive additional ones. A number of ombuds institutions have an explicit mandate to contribute to the fight against corruption. This most often happens in Africa, where, for instance, the ombuds institutions of Lesotho, Mauritius, Namibia, Rwanda, and South Africa (Public Protector) all have mandates to fight corruption. Ombuds institutions have also increasingly been designated as the external bodies for the protection of whistleblowers. The case of the Croatian Ombudsman is particularly notable, as the Law on the Protection of Persons Reporting Irregularities from 2019 explicitly designated the Ombudsman as an external reporting instance for whistleblowers (Art. 21). The Venice Principles note that ombuds institutions should give particular attention and protection to whistleblowers within the public sector (Venice Commission 2019: para. 16).

In many countries, under applicable international human rights conventions, ombuds institutions have been designated as, or as part of, a National Preventive Mechanism against Torture (NPM), under the Optional Protocol to the UN Convention against Torture (OPCAT), and/or Independent Monitoring Mechanism (IMM), under the UN Convention on the Rights of Persons with Disabilities (CRPD).

The OPCAT and CRPD do not prescribe any specific structure or model for independent monitoring mechanisms. Each state is free to choose its own model, taking into account its own national context and institutional architecture. Monitoring mechanisms could be a new, specialized body or an existing institution taking on the role. To illustrate, in the case of NPMs, several models have emerged. As seen below, in most of them, ombuds institutions play the key role:

- creating a new and specialized body on torture prevention (e.g., France, Germany, Italy, Tunisia);
- designating a national human rights commission (e.g., Turkey, Uruguay, Maldives, Morocco, Lebanon) or ombuds institution (e.g., Spain, Poland, Montenegro);
- designating an ombuds institution with formal involvement of civil society organizations (e.g., Serbia, Slovenia, Ukraine);
- designating an ombuds institution with formal involvement of specific regional NPM Commissions (e.g., Austria);
- designating several institutions to serve the purpose of the NPM (e.g., United Kingdom, Brazil, Argentina).

Good governance and principles of good (security sector) governance

There is no universally accepted definition of governance that would provide a convenient device for organizing the literature (Keefer 2009; Weiss 2000). Governance can be understood both as a system and a process. It is the system of values, policies, and institutions by which a society manages its economic, political, and social affairs through interactions within and among the state, civil society, and private sector. It includes the mechanisms and processes for citizens and groups to articulate their interests, mediate their differences, and exercise their legal rights and obligations (UNDP 2011). As a process, it refers to the formation of formal and informal rules that regulate the public realm (Hyden et al. 2004: 16). As noted by Addink (2014: 29), governance is an act of governing; it relates to decisions that define expectations, grant power, or verify performance that has legal consequences, and factual acts.

Good governance adds a normative or evaluative attribute to the process of governing (Gisselquist 2012). Both governance and good governance have been criticized for their lack of theoretical utility. UN OHCHR (2007: 2) defines good governance as the exercise of authority through political and institutional processes that are transparent and accountable, and encourage public participation. To that end, good governance is linked to the development of regulatory frameworks that guide a 'manner' for government actions, showing a specific way in which powers are exercised by the government (Castro 2019: 30).

Together with rule of law and democracy, good governance is one of the main cornerstones of the modern constitutional state. Those three are interconnected, as they 'make up the structure of the state and its institutions, the position of the governmental institutions and the citizens, and the norms for the relation between the government and the citizens' (Addink 2019a: 3).

How does one know if governance is good governance? What makes 'good governance'? In answering these questions, the focus here should be not on different, individual acts of governance (governance), but rather on the different principles as the overarching steering mechanisms for these activities (the principles of good governance) (Addink 2019a: 18).

Principles can be defined, in general terms, as 'goal norms' (Castro 2019: 153). Principles are future-looking norms as they establish a state of affairs that needs to be built. Principles are optimization requirements (Alexy 2010: 47–48), and immediate finalistic norms that describe an ideal state of affairs to be promoted (Avila 2007: 35–36). Compared to principles, rules are immediate descriptive norms that describe behaviors (Avila 2007: 36). Principles require more specific rules and procedures to operate. Principles may function to assemble or intermediate conflicting ideas. Likewise, principles generate and provide validity to the norms that operationalize them. Therefore, principles need rules to operate, and in turn provide the rationale for these rules (Botchway 2001: 182).

The realization of the ideal state of affairs requires the adoption of certain behaviors. These behaviors or conducts represent the means required in order to reach the state of affairs. On the other hand, the absence of these conducts hinders the realization of the state of affairs set by the norm as ideal, and consequently prevents the purpose from being reached (Castro 2019: 153–154). Such conducts 'become practical needs whose effects are needed to progressively advance to the purpose' (Ávila 2007: 41). Therefore, principles impose the duty of adopting the behaviors required, even if indirectly or regressively, to realize a state of affairs. In this regard, it is said that principles have a deontic-teleological character (Castro 2019: 154). They can be considered deontic because they set forth reasons for the existence of obligations, permissions, or prohibitions. They are teleological because obligations, permissions, and prohibitions stem from the effects of a given behavior that preserves or advances a certain state of affairs (Ávila 2007: 35).

At higher levels, good governance can be established as a legal norm in terms of constitutional principles. In this regard, it is important to keep in mind the difference between good governance and principles of good governance. As Addink (2014: 31) has pointed out, 'the principles of good governance have a strong normative connotation and may function mainly instrumentally, whereas good governance is the underlying concept and the consequence of the observance of the principles'. This implies that good governance also aims towards a goal and thus represents an end in itself. Therefore, good governance has an axiological dimension and constitutes a fundamental value (Castro 2019: 31).

The principles of good governance are the legal parameters for different kinds of government activities associated with the fulfilment of public tasks oriented to the citizens' well-being and the efficiency of the government. These principles are oriented to the good functioning of the entire state apparatus from the perspective of the democratic rule of law (Castro 2019: 32).

Before concentrating on the principles of good governance, one additional distinction is needed here – between good governance and good administration. Good governance is essential for the effective functioning of any administration. It provides a framework of principles that guide administrative actions and ensure the proper exercise of power. These principles serve as norms for administrative behavior and can be applied to promote good administration or protect individuals' rights. When implemented, they contribute to making sound decisions and maintaining a balance between safeguarding citizens' rights and advancing the general interest.

The concept of good administration encompasses the performance of administrative activities, adherence to best practices, and compliance with legal requirements. It emphasizes the need for transparency, accountability, participation, and responsiveness in administrative processes. Good administration is characterized by the responsible use of discretionary powers, which involves making decisions that are fair, reasonable, and in line with established norms and objectives. On the other hand, the absence of good administration leads to maladministration, which refers to administrative actions that fall short of the expected standards. Maladministration can include actions that are unjust, arbitrary, or in violation of individuals' rights. It represents a failure to uphold the principles of good governance and can undermine public trust in the administration.

Overall, good administration is a manifestation of good governance at the administrative level. By adhering to the principles of good governance, administrations can ensure effective and accountable decision-making processes, protect citizens' rights, and work towards the collective well-being of society.

Principles of good (security sector) governance

What makes the principles of good governance? It is hard to find two identical classifications of the principles of good governance. This was perfectly captured by Louis Meuleman, Rapporteur for the UN Committee of Experts on Public Administration (2019):

> How does one know when countries have implemented good governance? Although a cornerstone of all developmental efforts and the *sine qua non* of sustainability, governance is often nebulous. As a concept, it is hard to decipher. As a practice, it is hard to pin down. We can debate endlessly over the different elements that can go into its conceptual foundations. We can apply all kinds of elaborate models of analysis to get to the bottom of it. All efforts will surely and squarely lead to our pure dazzlement by the richness of its multifarious applications around the world.

Indeed, classifying and defining the principles of good governance is a challenging task. However, it does not mean that such an exercise is futile or counterproductive *per se*. It helps one to better understand the true nature of governance and what constitutes good governance.

International organizations, development agencies, and scholars have all offered different classifications of the principles of good governance. Table 2 lays down the principles most frequently referenced in the literature.

Table 2: Most usual principles of good governance with sources.

Principle (alphabetically)	Source (chronologically)
accountability	UNDP (1997), Graham (2003), CoE (2008), Lockwood (2010), DCAF (2015), Keping (2018), Castro (2019), Addink (2019a), Pomeranz and Stedman (2020)
capability	Lockwood (2010), Pomeranz and Stedman (2020)
competence	CoE (2008)
consensus-oriented	UNDP (1997)
direction	Graham (2003), Pomeranz and Stedman (2020)
effectiveness	UNDP (1997), CoE (2008), DCAF (2015), Keping (2018), Castro (2019), Addink (2019a)
efficiency	UNDP (1997), CoE (2008), DCAF (2015)
equity	UNDP (1997)
ethical conduct	CoE (2008)
fairness	Graham (2003), Lockwood (2010), Pomeranz and Stedman (2020)
human rights	CoE (2008), Addink (2019a)
inclusiveness	Lockwood (2010), Pomeranz and Stedman (2020)
innovation and openness to change	CoE (2008)
legitimacy	Graham (2003), Lockwood (2010), Keping (2018), Pomeranz and Stedman (2020)
participation	UNDP (1997), CoE (2008), DCAF (2015), Castro (2019), Addink (2019a)
performance	Graham (2003), Pomeranz and Stedman (2020)
properness	Castro (2019), Addink (2019a)
responsiveness	UNDP (1997), CoE (2008), DCAF (2015), Keping (2018)
rule of law	UNDP (1997), CoE (2008), DCAF (2015), Keping (2018)
sound financial management	CoE (2008)
strategic vision	UNDP (1997)
sustainability and long-term orientation	CoE (2008)
transparency	UNDP (1997), CoE (2008), Lockwood (2010), DCAF (2015), Keping (2018), Castro (2019), Addink (2019a), Pomeranz and Stedman (2020)

Initial attempts to determine and classify principles of good governance came from the international (development) community, not from scholars. The United Nations Development Program's 1997 report entitled 'Governance and Sustainable Human Development' (UNDP 1997) enunciates a set of principles that, with slight variations, appear in much of later literature.

As shown in the table, transparency, participation, responsiveness, efficiency, effectiveness, rule of law, and accountability are recognized in a vast majority of classifications. Some principles, such as properness, capability, or fairness, are recognized by some classifications but subsumed or named differently in some others.

The context that gave birth to some of those classifications should be considered. For instance, the 12 Principles of Good Democratic Governance were adopted in 2008 by the Council of Europe as part of the Strategy for Innovation and Good Governance at the Local Level. The Strategy and the Principles were agreed upon earlier at the 2007 Ministerial Conference in Valencia and endorsed by a decision of the Committee of Ministers of the Council of Europe in 2008. Although the 12 Principles as 'a reference point can help public authorities at any level measure and improve the quality of their governance and enhance service delivery to citizens' (Tatarenko n.d.), their focus on the local level led the drafter to include some principles not usually found in similar exercises, such as sound financial management, or innovation and openness to change.

Finally, some classifications disaggregate principles into their constituent parts/sub-components. That is the case for one set of principles designed particularly for good governance in the development context. In 2018, The United Nations Committee of Experts on Public Administration (CEPA), established by the Economic and Social Council (ECOSOC), formulated the Principles of Effective Governance for Sustainable Development, intending to organically integrate good governance into the implementation of the 2030 Agenda for Sustainable Development so that no one is left behind.

The Committee recognized three main principles – effectiveness, accountability, and inclusiveness, which were then divided into a total of 11 sub-principles (Table 3).

Table 3: Principles of effective governance for sustainable development (UN ECOSOC 2018).

Main category	No.	Principle
Effectiveness	1.	competence
	2.	sound policy making
	3.	collaboration
Accountability	4.	integrity
	5.	transparency
	6.	independent oversight
Inclusiveness	7.	leaving no one behind
	8.	non-discrimination
	9.	participation
	10.	subsidiarity
	11.	intergenerational equity

Some of the principles that stand alone in Table 3, such as transparency or participation, have been subsumed in the CEPA's classification by these three main categories. In contrast, in some other classifications, inclusiveness is subsumed by participation, whilst responsiveness is consumed by accountability. It is, thus, duly noted that these principles often overlap or even conflict at some point; they play out in practice according to the actual social context; applying such principles is complex; and they concern not only the results of power, but how well it is exercised (Graham, Amos & Plumptre 2003).

After comparing and contrasting these different categories, this study opted for the adoption of the classification of the principles of good (security sector) governance as proposed by DCAF – the Geneva Centre for Security Sector Governance (2015), to include: (1) accountability, (2) rule of law, (3) transparency, (4) participation, (5) responsiveness, (6) effectiveness, and (7) efficiency. This classification contains key principles featured in almost all attempts to grasp good governance. It is both comprehensive and avoids duplications. DCAF's classification is created for a specific context of SSG/R, which is of particular relevance for this study, which attempts to connect ombuds institutions, SDGs, and the security sector. With the emphasis on participation and responsiveness, it covers the central *credo* of the 2030 Agenda, to leave no one behind, whilst with the inclusion of the principles of accountability, rule of law and transparency, it directly relates with SDG 16, aiming at achieving accountable and just institutions.

It should be noted that the principles of good governance do not always aim in the same direction; there are issues concerning their mutual relationship, and they do not yet have a univocal meaning (Addink 2019b: 7). With this in mind, this research uses the following definitions of the seven aforementioned principles.

Accountability de facto constraints the government's use of political power through requirements for justification of its actions and potential sanctions by both citizens and oversight institutions (Lührmann, Marquardt, and Mechkova 2020: 812). It means that administrators and administrative bodies must fulfil the functions and obligations of the positions they hold. If they fail to fulfil their bounden functions or duties, or if they do so in an inappropriate manner, their conduct constitutes dereliction of duty or lack of accountability (Keping 2018). In the context of the security sector, accountability refers to clear expectations for security provision, and independent authorities oversee whether these expectations are met and impose sanctions if they are not met.

Essentially, rule of law means that law is the supreme observed by all government officials and citizens, who should all be equal before the law. All persons and institutions, including the state, are subject to laws that are publicly known, enforced impartially, and consistent with international and national human rights norms and standards.

Transparency means that information is freely available and accessible to those who will be affected by decisions and their implementation (DCAF 2015).

Participation means that people of all backgrounds have the opportunity to take part in decision-making and service provision on a free, equitable, and inclusive basis, either directly or through legitimate representative institutions (DCAF 2015). Inclusiveness is here subsumed by participation. Inclusiveness means that institutions promote participatory empowerment of citizens, and invest efforts in including all individuals and groups, specifically individuals or groups who were previously not included or excluded. This goes along with the appreciation of diversity in personal characteristics. The term inclusive suggests that individuals have equal access to the social, political, and economic mainstream (Dörffel & Schuhmann 2022).

Responsiveness indicates that public institutions serve all stakeholders and respond to the demands of citizens in a timely and responsible manner. Institutions are sensitive to the different security needs of all parts of the population and perform their missions in the spirit of a culture of service.

Effectiveness means that institutions fulfil their respective roles, responsibilities, and missions to a high professional standard.

Finally, efficiency implies that institutions make the best possible use of public resources in fulfilling their respective roles, responsibilities, and missions.

Connecting good governance, human rights, security, and development

This chapter deals with four concepts that could all be labeled as 'essentially contested' (Baldwin 1997: 10; Gallie 1956) and can only be defined in general terms: good governance, human rights, security, and development. The relationship between any two of these four concepts has been widely described as 'a nexus' in the literature. Here, a nexus is understood as 'a network of connections between disparate ideas, processes or objects; alluding to a nexus implies an infinite number of possible linkages and relations' (Stern & Öjendal 2010: 11). This chapter does not attempt to provide any grand definitions of these concepts but to lay down how these interrelated concepts are understood and used in this study. It starts with the nexus between good governance and human rights, then it focuses on human rights and development, turning to governance and development, and closes with security and development.

There is an intrinsic link between good governance and human rights. As shown in the previous chapter, some authors have included human rights as one of the principles of good governance. Regarding the latter, the right to good administration has been increasingly recognized, most notably through Article 41 of the Charter of Fundamental Rights of the European Union. From a human rights perspective, good governance refers primarily to the process whereby public institutions conduct public affairs, manage public resources, and guarantee the realization of human rights. As further argued by OHCHR (n.d.):

> The true test of 'good' governance is the degree to which it delivers on the promise of human rights. Human rights standards and principles provide a set of values to guide the work of governments and other political and social actors. They also provide a set of performance standards against which these actors can be held accountable. Moreover, human rights principles inform the content of good governance efforts: they may inform the development of legislative frameworks, policies, programmes, budgetary allocations and other measures. On the other hand, without good governance, human rights cannot be respected and protected in a sustainable manner. The implementation of human rights relies on a conducive and enabling environment. This includes appropriate legal frameworks and institutions as well as political, managerial and administrative processes responsible for responding to the rights and needs of the population.

Human rights norms and good governance norms can only be realized by each other, in the sense that human rights need good governance and good governance needs human rights (Addink 2019a: 173). The interaction between good governance and human rights has already been established in international and domestic law. For example, some principles of good governance, such as transparency or participation, can be found in the sources of international human rights law (Table 4). The principles of participation and transparency have been embedded in the right to access information, as stipulated by the European Convention on Human Rights (Hins & Voorhoof 2007).

Table 4: Articles from international treaties in which the principles of good governance have been reflected.

Principle/treaty	UDHR	ICCPR	ECHR
participation	6, 8, 14(1), 21(1), 29(2)	6, 9(4), 13, 16, 25	15, 22
transparency		8, 40ff	10
accountability	30	1, 5, 40ff	19ff
effectiveness	22, 25(1)		5(2,3), 13,17

Note: Universal Declaration of Human Rights (UDHR), International Covenant on Civil and Political Rights (ICCPR), and European Convention on Human Rights (ECHR).

Good governance and human rights are thus mutually reinforcing, although characterized by many tensions. The same applies to the nexus between human rights and security. As observed by Jenkins-Smith and Herron (2009: 1096), tensions between civil liberties and security measures are sometimes mistakenly cast in zero-sum terms, suggesting that gains in security and order necessarily come at the expense of freedom and liberty, or that increasing freedom always diminishes security. Indeed, the relationship between security and liberty (human rights) is better understood as symbiotic rather than conflicting. Although many political regimes try to promote the view that more security has to come at the expense of the rights of citizens, this is more an attempt to securitize, to use extraordinary measures, to move away from ordinary democratic procedures, with the goal to consolidate political power. Insisting on the principles of good governance serves to help prevent such attempts. Good security sector governance means that the security sector should be held to the same high standards of public service delivery as other public sector service providers (DCAF 2015).

The link between human rights and development has also been well recognized ever since the 1986 Declaration on the Right to Development. There are strong reasons for much systemic integration of human rights into development policy and practice. Mcinerney-Lankford (2009:52) offers three. First, they are intrinsically valuable in aiming to protect human dignity (e.g., *jus cogens*) and may be (negatively) affected by development so development policy should identify ways to, at a minimum, meet the 'do no harm' threshold. Second, they are also instrumentally useful to enhance development processes, address certain types of social risk, ensure accountability, and ultimately secure more equitable and sustainable development outcomes. Third, as a matter of public international law, human rights treaty obligations are legally binding, and under custom bind all states other than persistent objectors; as such they should be respected in all contexts, including development.

Similar to the case of the nexus between good governance and human rights, the principles of good governance are also the tenets of the development policy. Principles such as participation, inclusiveness, and accountability are well established in development discourse. As early as 2001, the UN Independent Expert on the Right to Development, Arjun Sengupta, in his report to the UN Commission on Human Rights, asserted that the right to development is a vector of all human rights, and emphasized 'the realization of each human right and all of them together has to be carried out in a rights-based manner, as a participatory, accountable and transparent process with equity in decision-making and sharing of the fruits of the process while maintaining respect for civil and political rights' (Sengupta 2001: 21).

The United Nations have indeed been at the forefront of efforts to establish stronger links between human rights and development. The so-called rights-based approach to development (HRBA) is mandated as integral to the form and content of the UN's development policy (UNSDG 2003). Despite these efforts, the relationship between human rights and development today is defined more by its distinctions and disconnects. Some authors recognize the deep tension between presenting moral ambitions in the language of (human) rights and presenting them in the language of (development) goals, as a first and most fundamental concern. Pogge and Sengupta (2016: 2) argue that the development goals discourse invites an incremental approach to overcoming deprivations, while the human rights discourse suggests that deprivations must be ended right away. When severe deprivations constitute unfulfilled human rights – and, given their social origins, even human rights violations – then they categorically require immediate and top-priority remedial attention (Pogge and Sengupta 2016: 2). The same authors criticize the UN language of 'progressive realization,' as it indicates that the full eradication of various deprivations recognized by the SDGs may take as much time as the governments deem reasonable to complete the task (Pogge and Sengupta 2016: 3).

If one problem is the pace of 'progressive realization,' another one is the generalist and abstract inclusion of human rights into development policy at the level of principles, perspectives, or considerations, rather than obligations. Often the references to human rights instruments are put either in a preambular way or in general terms. Consequently, human rights become part of the general policy narrative but rarely are the legal ramifications of specific instruments articulated in development policies that reference them, potentially limiting the degree to which human rights can be integrated (Mcinerney-Lankford 2009: 58–59). For these reasons, many scholars and practitioners have advocated for an international convention on the right to development. The drafting process is already in an advanced stage (Teshome 2022). As with other similar conventions, the drafting process is characterized by a struggle to resolve theoretical ideality and the political reality, that is, to reconcile expert views with the political standpoints of Member States. While the UN Convention on the Right to Development should contribute to closing the gap between human rights and development, the same process has also reiterated the importance of the nexus between governance and development.

As famously noted by former United Nations Secretary-General Kofi Annan, 'good governance is perhaps the single most important factor in eradicating poverty and promoting development' (UN 1998). Many studies have focused on measures and assessments of governance quality, either in individual countries or cross-nationally (Apaza 2009; Arndt & Oman 2006; Besançon 2003), and the relationship between governance and main outcomes such as economic growth (Holmberg, Rothstein & Nasiritousi 2009; Kaufmann, Kraay & Zoido-Lobatón 1999; Keefer 2009;). However, an increasing body of literature questions the causal effect of the quality of governance on various outcomes, particularly economic growth (Kurtz & Schrank 2007a; 2007b). Some authors, such as Grindle (2004), also raise a similar argument as is the case with the nexus between human rights and development, pointing out that the good governance agenda is a poor guide for policy because it is *ad hoc*, 'unrealistically long', and not attuned to issues of sequencing and historical development.

Given the ambiguities of the concepts of governance and good governance, it seems more potent to concentrate on the disaggregated components or principles of good governance, rather than on good governance as the *ad hoc* macro concept (Gisselquist 2012: 2), or the meta-concept (Addink 2019a: 19). Such a focus on the disaggregation of the concept should allow for more precision in the formulation (Gisselquist 2012: 2). For these reasons, the study accepts the principle-led approach, as already indicated. The same applies to the relationship between security and development to a large extent.

Today, the importance of the nexus between security and development is well established in the literature and among practitioners. However, historically, notions of 'security' and 'development' emerge from disparate ontologies. In the colonial era, attention to 'security' was a pinnacle of much 'development' strategy, whilst the Marshall Plan offers an example of 'development' concerns as central to Western security policies. Since the end of the Cold War, security and development concerns have been increasingly interlinked. As noted by Chandler (2007: 362–363), 'since the end of the 1990s, and particularly after 9/11, the framework of the "security-development nexus" has been hailed as a way of cohering national and international policy-making interventions in non-Western states.'

Two major factors contribute to such a change. Firstly, development was no longer equated with economic growth. Secondly, the rise of the human security concept within the development community has provided a rich playground for a more comprehensive understanding of both security and development (Dursun-Özkanca 2021; Khagram, Clark & Firas Raad 2003). The policy documents started to talk about the joining of practices and theories in these two policy areas as a way of creating a 'joined-up government' or of facilitating multilateral intervention under new 'holistic', 'coherent', or 'comprehensive' approaches to non-Western states (Chandler 2007: 362–363).

This process also included adding the prefix 'sustainable' to development, recognizing that development is not an exclusively positive notion. It may indeed bring negative effects on nature, human development, and human rights.

The security apparatus is increasingly involved in large-scale development projects, particularly when such projects do not enjoy the support of the local community. Sometimes, they are employed to clear the terrain, in other places to enforce expropriation, elsewhere to keep protesters away, or even run the projects themselves. Understood in narrow terms and applied selectively, security and development may indeed contribute to authoritarian tendencies. To make development sustainable, good governance and human rights have to be added to the equation. This essentially means guiding the development by the principles of good governance and good security sector governance.

As in the case of good governance and development, it was again Kofi Annan that has acted as the key proponent of a strong nexus between security and development, arguing:

> Development and security are inextricably linked. A more secure world is only possible if poor countries are given a real chance to develop. Extreme poverty and infectious diseases threaten many people directly, but they also provide a fertile breeding ground for other threats, including civil conflicts (UN 2004: vii).

This citation depicts the richness of the link(s) between security and development, uniting different historical trajectories, approaches, and narratives. As demonstrated by Stern and Öjendal (2010: 22), references to 'a more secure world' draw upon the framing of 'globalized security-development,' which arguably lends legitimacy and urgency to the call for 'giving the poor countries a real chance to develop' as the only viable way out of the implied 'insecure' world in which we now live. The threats emanating from 'extreme poverty' arguably draw upon the 'broadening, deepening and humanizing' discourse in its depiction of human insecurities and symptoms of arrested human development or underdevelopment. The citation then shifts to the 'modern teleological narrative' as a source for presenting the scenario of 'other threats,' civil conflicts, and the violence and destruction they wreak (Stern and Öjendal 2010: 23). These authors see the depiction of a 'fertile breeding ground for threats' as evoking the image of the political body/society as an infested wound, which must be cured of its 'germs' for it to be secure (Stern and Öjendal 2010: 23). This part of the quote brings in an understanding of security as a 'technique of governmentality' (Stern and Öjendal 2010: 23).

Building on this comprehensive understanding of the security-development nexus, the next chapter adds ombuds institutions to the equation, by presenting the methodological framework for a better understanding of the role of these institutions in achieving the SDGs, particularly SDG 16, in the context of SSG/R.

CHAPTER 3

Analyzing the Role of Ombuds Institutions in Achieving SDG 16

The relationship between SSG/R and SDG 16 has recently caught the attention of scholarly and policy communities. Scholars have sought to explore the conceptual links between the two, whilst policy advisors have looked into ways to operationalize SDG 16 in the context of peacebuilding and democratic consolidation. For scholars, the critical question has been to examine the fabric of this relationship. Oya Dursun-Özkanca (2021) sees human security as the most potent framework for understanding the nexus between SSG/R and SDG 16. She argues that 'human security's emphasis on reforming security and justice sectors and on accountability, oversight, and participative approach and local ownership can facilitate the accomplishment of SDG 16's primary objective of establishing peace, justice, and strong and inclusive institutions' (Dursun-Özkanca 2021: 66).

This chapter builds on these discussions, by concentrating on accountability, oversight, and local ownership. It starts with an overview of the 2030 Agenda and the SDGs, before concentrating on SDG 16. It then introduces the role of ombuds institutions as security sector actors and development actors, respectively. To be able to better understand and critically assess the role of ombuds institutions in realizing SDG 16, this chapter moves on to develop a methodological framework. The aim is to determine whether and how ombuds institutions could contribute to the achievement of each of the 12 SDG 16 targets. Given the comprehensive nature and complexity of those targets and indicators, this chapter presents the framework conceptualized by linking the principles of SSG, key roles of ombuds institutions/NHRIs in achieving SDGs, and the SDG 16 targets.

Sustainable Development Goal 16

The SDGs, the centerpiece of the 2030 Agenda for Sustainable Development, were adopted by the United Nations Sustainable Development Summit in September 2015. The 2030 Agenda builds upon the expiring MDGs: eight targets that guided global action on the reduction of extreme

How to cite this book chapter:
Glušac, L. 2023. *Leaving No One Behind, Leaving No One Unaccountable: Ombuds Institutions, Good (Security Sector) Governance and Sustainable Development Goal 16*. Pp. 25–36. London: Ubiquity Press. DOI: https://doi.org/10.5334/bcw.c. License: CC BY-NC 4.0

poverty in its multiple dimensions from 2000 to 2015. Whilst the SDGs maintain the thematic work on poverty eradication targeted by the MDGs, they reflect a comprehensive perspective on international development and sustaining human life on this planet.

World leaders have recognized that:

> Eradicating poverty in all its forms and dimensions, including extreme poverty, is the greatest global challenge and an indispensable requirement for sustainable development. All countries and all stakeholders, acting in collaborative partnership, will implement this plan. We are resolved to free the human race from the tyranny of poverty and want and to heal and secure our planet (2030 Agenda).

They have pledged 'that no one will be left behind' and promised to 'take the bold and transformative steps which are urgently needed to shift the world onto a sustainable and resilient path.'

Contrary to the MDGs which only applied to developing countries, the SDGs apply universally to all UN Member States and are considerably more comprehensive and ambitious than the MDGs. The road to having SDGs applicable to all Member States, irrespective of their level of development, was extremely difficult to negotiate. As argued by Caballero (2019: 138), 'the proposition that a truly universal agenda was needed brought to the surface assumptions that were implicit in development assistance – that development was only actionable by so-called developing countries and that the responsibilities of the more developed countries were only to provide limited finance and-often patriarchic-assistance.' It was the creation of the Open Working Group (OWG) that made the ultimate adoption of the universal agenda possible, because this format allowed for inclusive and transparent discussions, without being restricted by the formal rules of the UN General Assembly if it operated as an 'open-ended' working group. It created a unique space for effective, active participation not just by all countries, but by all major stakeholders, and also enabled the Group to be highly technocratic, with the participation of both invited experts as well as those that delegations soon began to bring in from their own capitals (Caballero 2019: 138).

The 2030 Agenda contains 17 global goals (Table 5) and 169 targets, with a total of 248 indicators. The development of targets and indicators was also a long and tiresome process. While operating in the OWG brought a surprisingly high level of presence and influence of science and technical experts in formulating SDGs, as a tradeoff, the process of defining indicators – which would normally have been technical – became much politicized. Hence, it was through the very complex process of several rounds of consultations between national statistician experts, government representatives, UN agencies, and civil society organizations (CSOs) that the indicators were ultimately formulated.

Fukuda-Parr distinguishes between the governance effects and the knowledge effects of global goals. In terms of governance, the broad policy purpose of global goals is to put issues on the agenda and to increase attention and support for areas that are important for development but have thus far been neglected (Fukuda-Parr 2014: 119). Goals are intended to promote changes in policy and implementation at the national level by creating incentives (Fukuda-Parr 2014: 120). In this regard, global monitoring has been used for performance evaluation, as an accountability framework, and as a basis for advocacy (Fukuda-Parr 2014: 122–123). In addition to the governance effects, the knowledge effects must be considered. Target setting – and the indicators associated with targets – have the potential to influence how norms themselves are defined and understood and how the narrative around their implementation is shaped (Fukuda-Parr 2014: 120). Merry (2011: S92) has argued that 'indicators produce readily understandable and convenient forms of knowledge about the world that shape the way policymakers and the general public understand the world.' The formulation and framing of the targets, indicators, and their

Table 5: The 17 Sustainable Development Goals.

Sustainable Development Goals
Goal 1. End poverty in all its forms everywhere.
Goal 2. End hunger, achieve food security and improved nutrition and promote sustainable agriculture.
Goal 3. Ensure healthy lives and promote well-being for all at all ages.
Goal 4. Ensure inclusive and equitable quality education and promote lifelong learning opportunities for all.
Goal 5. Achieve gender equality and empower all women and girls.
Goal 6. Ensure availability and sustainable management of water and sanitation for all.
Goal 7. Ensure access to affordable, reliable, sustainable and modern energy for all.
Goal 8. Promote sustained, inclusive and sustainable economic growth, full and productive employment and decent work for all.
Goal 9. Build resilient infrastructure, promote inclusive and sustainable industrialization and foster innovation.
Goal 10. Reduce inequality within and among countries.
Goal 11. Make cities and human settlements inclusive, safe, resilient and sustainable.
Goal 12. Ensure sustainable consumption and production patterns.
Goal 13. Take urgent action to combat climate change and its impacts.
Goal 14. Conserve and sustainably use the oceans, seas and marine resources for sustainable development.
Goal 15. Protect, restore and promote sustainable use of terrestrial ecosystems, sustainably manage forests, combat desertification, and halt and reverse land degradation and halt biodiversity loss.
Goal 16. Promote peaceful and inclusive societies for sustainable development, provide access to justice for all and build effective, accountable, and inclusive institutions at all levels.
Goal 17. Strengthen the means of implementation and revitalize the global partnership for sustainable development.

disaggregation have a significant influence on what data governments and development partners will gather over the next 15 years or more and 'what matters' in the implementation of the Sustainable Development Agenda (CESR 2016: 33).

SDG 16 stresses the need for strong institutions that are built on respect for human rights, effective rule of law, and good governance at all levels (DCAF 2021). It is arguably one of the most ambitious goals in the 2030 Agenda because it is not simply a goal by itself but also an enabler for the achievement of other goals. However, many SDG 16 targets are rather vague, and limited guidance exists on how to measure and achieve them, especially in fragile contexts (DCAF 2021).

Under the Sustainable Development Goal 16, the United Nations have defined 10 targets to be achieved by 2030, shown in Table 6.

Besides these 10 'regular' targets, SDG 16 includes two targets described as 'means of implementation' (MoI), raising the total number of targets to 12, shown in Table 7.

The UN defines the notion of 'means of implementation' as 'the interdependent mix of financial resources, technology development and transfer, capacity-building, inclusive and equitable globalization and trade, regional integration, as well as the creation of a national enabling environment required to implement the new sustainable development agenda, particularly in developing countries' (TST n.d.). The MoI targets were introduced late in the process of negotiation of the SDGs and provided a way to accommodate some of the concerns of Member States regarding how the SDGs were to be achieved (Bartram et al. 2018).

Table 6: The 10 main SDG 16 targets.

No.	Target
16.1	Significantly reduce all forms of violence and related death rates everywhere.
16.2	End abuse, exploitation, trafficking and all forms of violence against and torture of children.
16.3	Promote the rule of law at the national and international levels and ensure equal access to justice for all.
16.4	By 2030, significantly reduce illicit financial and arms flows, strengthen the recovery and return of stolen assets and combat all forms of organised crime.
16.5	Substantially reduce corruption and bribery in all their forms.
16.6	Develop effective, accountable and transparent institutions at all levels.
16.7	Ensure responsive, inclusive, participatory and representative decision-making at all levels.
16.8	Broaden and strengthen the participation of developing countries in the institutions of global governance.
16.9	By 2030, provide legal identity for all, including birth registration.
16.10	Ensure public access to information and protect fundamental freedoms, in accordance with national legislation and international agreements.

Table 7: The two SDG 16 'means of implementation' targets.

No.	'Means of implementation' target
16.A	Strengthen relevant national institutions, including through international cooperation, for building capacity at all levels, in particular in developing countries, to prevent violence and combat terrorism and crime.
16.B	Promote and enforce non-discriminatory laws and policies for sustainable development.

Many of these targets directly relate to the security sector. This particularly applies to targets 16.1, 16.2, and 16.4, aiming at reducing all forms of violence, ending abuse, exploitation, trafficking, and torture; reducing illicit financial and arms flows, strengthening the recovery and return of stolen assets; and combating all forms of organized crime, respectively.

Several SDG 16 targets promote good governance and may be directly applied to good security sector governance as well. Targets 16.3, 16.6, and 16.7 all aim to promote, develop, and ensure the principles of good governance, by emphasizing the need for effective, accountable, transparent, responsive, inclusive, and participatory institutions and decision-making. Finally, some of the targets, such as 16.2, 16.5, and 16.8, focus on protecting human rights and fundamental freedoms, as well as suppressing corruption.

To operationalize and contextualize this goal, a growing number of countries produce their own versions of Goal 16 (UNDP 2017). Laberge and Touihri (2019: 154) have convincingly shown that 'by translating the abstract concepts contained in global SDG 16 targets into the language of issues that are currently being contested in a given country, such exercises can overcome some of the distortions or "slippage in ambition" that have plagued indicator selection processes at global level and can incentivize action by policymakers.' They have used the Tunisian case to demonstrate how national SDG 16 indicators, when jointly defined by state and non-state actors and publicly monitored and disseminated, can emerge as a powerful 'currency' for governments to earn and retain public trust, and for society to hold it to account (Laberge and Touihri 2019: 154).

Furthermore, the Tunisians have put explicit emphasis on the promotion and protection of human rights, and a dedicated national indicator measuring people's perception of the extent to which fundamental rights and freedoms are respected in the country (Laberge and Touihri 2019: 154).

The National Human Rights Commission of Mongolia (NHRCM) has been actively engaged in a multi-stakeholder initiative aimed at developing national SDG indicators, promoting the message that 90 percent of the SDG targets reflect human rights obligations (DIHR 2020: 8). When the SDGs are promoted as human rights instruments, ombuds institutions may play a much bigger role, including by acting as information-provider, as in Georgia, where the indicator selection process relies on administrative data produced by, *inter alia*, the Office of the Public Defender (UNDP 2017: 14).

The examples of Mongolia and Georgia demonstrate that ombuds institutions' comprehensive mandate and the position in the overall governance structure of the state make them well suited to contribute to the realization of many SDG 16 targets. Before discussing this in more detail in the following chapters, ombuds' wider role as a security sector and development actor is explored.

Ombuds institutions as security sector actors

The SSR concept has gone through numerous transformations since its emergence among the donor and academic communities in the 1990s. It has evolved into a holistic and inclusive approach to the consolidation of democratic governance of the security sector (Glušac 2018b: 61). The actorness of ombuds institutions in SSR comes naturally, given that SSR is people-centered, locally owned, and based on democratic norms, human rights principles, and the rule of law (OECD 2007), aimed at 'the efficient and effective provision of state and human security within a framework of democratic governance' (Hänggi 2004: 3).

The widely adopted holistic approach to SSR distinguishes four groups of SSR actors (Figure 1) (Ball 1998; Edmunds 2002; Ejdus 2012: 64).

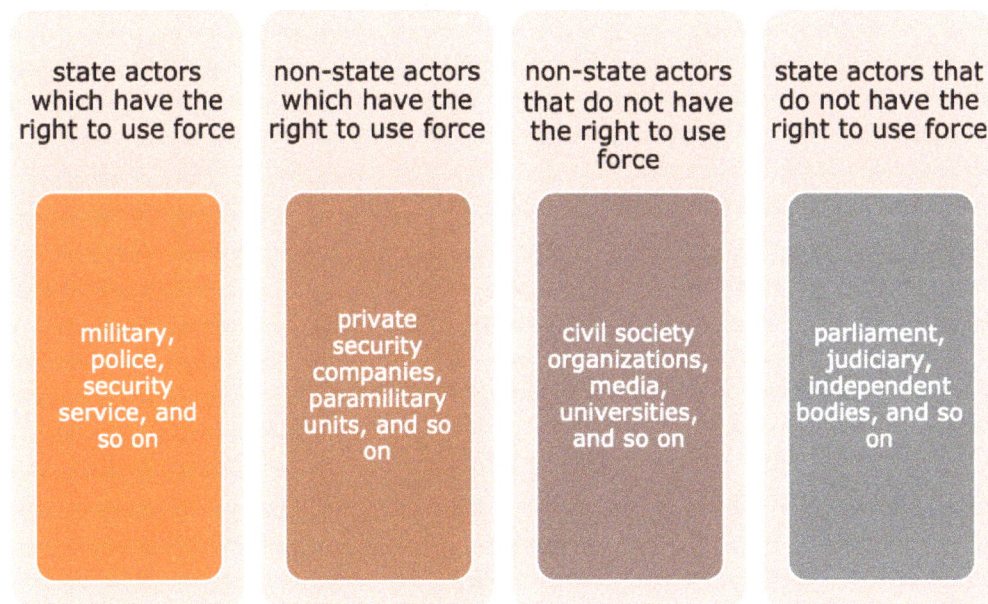

state actors which have the right to use force	non-state actors which have the right to use force	non-state actors that do not have the right to use force	state actors that do not have the right to use force
military, police, security service, and so on	private security companies, paramilitary units, and so on	civil society organizations, media, universities, and so on	parliament, judiciary, independent bodies, and so on

Figure 1: Four groups of SSR actors (Ejdus 2012: 64).

Ombuds institutions occupy a special position among state actors that do not have the right to use force (IPU & DCAF 2003: 89). This is due to their comprehensive mandate, investigative powers, and access to documents and premises of public authorities, including security institutions. Despite such understanding, empirical evidence on the activities of ombuds institutions in SSR is, with a few exceptions (Born & Wills 2012; Kinzelbach & Cole 2007), notably scarce. This applies even more when it comes to the case studies on oversight of the intelligence/security services (Glušac 2018b: 61). Scholarly literature on ombuds institutions and other forms of NHRIs also provides little information on their role in the oversight of the security sector. Even the most elaborate research on NHRIs has dealt with this topic only laterally (Cardenas 2014; Goodman & Pegram 2012; Wouters & Meuwissen 2013). The most promising strand of literature related to ombuds institutions in the context of the security sector has been the one focusing on the armed forces (Buckland & McDermott 2012; DCAF 2017; McDermott 2021).

Such a generally neglected status of ombuds institutions in the literature can be attributed to the rather modest successes of ombuds institutions and/or failure to advertise success stories (Glušac 2018b: 60). Indeed, comparative experiences have shown that ombuds institutions do not often exploit the possibility to effectively oversee the security sector to a full extent (Council of Europe Commissioner for Human Rights 2015). This is surprising, because, as argued by Janković (2006), these institutions are well-placed to: (1) make a substantial contribution to the effective protection of the human rights and freedoms of the citizens affected by the activities of security services; (2) reinforce and complete the framework for democratic civilian oversight; and (3) strengthen the democratic foundations underlying the operations of the services, thereby improving their work and consequently increasing the public's trust in them.

The United Nations sees independent oversight of the security sector as essential to ensuring accountability and strengthening confidence in its governance. In its publication on security sector reform, the UN (2012: 98) stated:

> A system of independent oversight should be created to provide clear and transparent channels for substantive dialogue and cooperation between oversight institutions and statutory security sector actors. Independent bodies with specialized mandates (i.e., national human rights institutions) perform vital roles in the governance of the security sector.

In the Council of Europe Commissioner for Human Rights' account of the role of European ombuds institutions in security sector oversight, it is noted that most do not play a significant role with regard to the oversight of security and intelligence services: 'In many countries, the possibility exists for an ombudsman to investigate complaints about the security services but they rarely do so in practice' (Council of Europe Commissioner for Human Rights 2015: 51). It is useful to add that in some countries, security and intelligence services are exempt from the ombuds' oversight. According to Kucsko-Stadlmayer (2008: 49–89), that applies in Belgium, the Czech Republic, France, Greece, Israel, Malta, and Slovakia. In these countries, separate specialized bodies have been established to exclusively oversee the security and intelligence services. It should be noted that a number of countries have specialized ombuds institutions, which focus exclusively on armed forces. That is the case, for instance, in Germany, Austria, Norway, Bosnia and Herzegovina, the United Kingdom, South Africa, and Canada.

In the case of NHRIs more generally, the Paris Principles do not mention the security sector specifically. Nevertheless, in its authoritative interpretation of the Paris Principles, SCA stated that the mandate of NHRIs should be interpreted in a broad, liberal, and purposive manner and that it should, *inter alia*, authorize a full investigation into all alleged human rights violations, including by military, police, and security officers (GANHRI SCA 2018). The SCA noted that the scope of the mandate of an NHRI may be restricted for national security reasons. However, it reiterated that 'while this limitation is not inherently contrary to the Paris Principles, it should not be unreasonably or arbitrarily applied and should only be exercised under due process' (G.O. 2.6.

GANHRI SCA 2018). Through its General Observations of the Paris Principles, the SCA has also covered the issue of operating in the situation of a coup d'état or a state of emergency. The SCA underlined:

> It is expected that an NHRI will conduct itself with a heightened level of vigilance and independence, and in strict accordance with its mandate. NHRIs are expected to promote and ensure respect for human rights, democratic principles and the strengthening of the rule of law in all circumstances and without exception. In situations of conflict or a state of emergency, this may include monitoring, documenting, issuing public statements and releasing regular and detailed reports through the media in a timely manner to address urgent human rights violations (G.O. 2.5. GANHRI SCA 2018).

Another relevant document on the security actorness of ombuds institutions and other NHRIs is the Kyiv Declaration from 2015, which lays down a number of potential roles they could have in conflict and post-conflict situations, including, *inter alia*, taking measures to identify early signs of possible conflict and steps to prevent conflict, including through addressing the violations of human rights; promoting a dialogue between and with conflicting parties aiming to ensure the promotion, protection, and respect of human rights; and taking steps to ensure human rights are placed at the center of negotiations between the conflicting parties, including in peace agreements, and monitor their implementation (ENNHRI 2015).

It is not easy to effectively oversee the security sector. A number of preconditions have to be met. Born and Geisler Mesevage (2012: 322) have laid down three – the ability to access relevant information, question intelligence/security officials, and issue findings and recommendations on the basis of what it learns. Still, ombuds institutions fulfil these three preconditions. These are also all recognized by the key standards for NHRIs, including by the Paris Principles (Glušac 2018b: 65).

Key internal preconditions for successful oversight are expert knowledge and institutional credibility (Glušac 2018b: 65–66). If ombudspersons do not have expert knowledge of security-related issues, experts should be employed to allow substantive activities to be included in their oversight. Carver (2012: 201) correctly observed that 'the security sector provides a particularly striking example of the difficulties of enforcing accountability.' It is thus necessary that an ombuds institution builds credibility, because, as suggested by Neave (2014: 31), their work is not derived from binding, coercive, or determinative powers, but from the rigor, objectivity, and independence with which they conduct their activities. Ombuds institutions are seen through the lenses of their mandate-holders. Hence, 'the role of individual leadership should not be overlooked, since many NHRIs—like any organization—thrive under the independent-mindedness or perseverance of particular commissioners or, alternatively, flounder in the face of passive leadership' (Cardenas 2014: 449). The success of ombuds institutions therefore 'depends overwhelmingly on the strength of their mandate-holder(s) and their ability to position themselves as an objective, rigorous and credible authority' (Glušac 2018b: 65–66). In other words, the effectiveness of an ombuds institution depends on the personal independence and impartiality of its leader and staff (DCAF 2017: 2).

Ombuds institutions as development/SDG actors

Scholarly literature has not devoted much attention to ombuds institutions as development actors. However, the adoption of the MDGs and particularly the SDGs has motivated the policy and practitioners' community to explore the potential of ombuds institutions to contribute to their realization. Through their fora, ombuds institutions have also initiated discussions and started to compare notes on what they can do (and how) to promote and contribute to the SDGs.

Several discussion papers, guidelines, and overviews of good practices have been published by GANHRI and its partners. This literature describes ombuds institutions in the context of the

SDGs in various terms, such as 'accelerators, guarantors and indicators of sustainable development' (DIHR & GANHRI 2019), 'credible data providers' (DIHR & GANHRI 2019), and 'bridges between stakeholders and promote transparent, participatory, and inclusive national processes of implementation and monitoring' (Mérida Declaration 2015: para. 15). How do these different roles play out in practice, and through which types of activities?

The most elaborated answer to these questions was given in the 2015 Mérida Declaration on the Role of National Human Rights Institutions in implementing the 2030 Agenda for Sustainable Development, adopted by GANHRI. The Mérida Declaration provides for the comprehensive set of functions and activities that ombuds institutions and other NHRIs can undertake in order to contribute to a human-rights-based approach to the 2030 Agenda and the realization of the SDGs (Table 8).

Table 8: The Mérida Declaration: NHRIs' functions and activities in the context of SDGs.

Function	Activity
Providing advice to national and local governments, rights-holders and other actors through	assessing the impact of laws, policies, programmes, national development plans, administrative practices and budgets on the realization of all human rights for all.
Developing and strengthening partnerships for implementation through	promoting transparent and inclusive processes for participation and consultation with rights-holders and civil society, such as the development of national and sub-national strategies to achieve the SDGs, including reaching out to those who are furthest behind.
Engaging with duty-bearers, rights-holders and other key actors by	raising awareness and building trust and promoting dialogue and concerted efforts for a human rights-based approach to implementation and monitoring of the Agenda, and safeguarding space for engagement of rightsholders and civil society.
Assisting in the shaping of global national indicators and sound data collection systems to ensure the protection and promotion of human rights in the measurement of the Agenda by	seeking collaboration with national statistical offices, where appropriate, and other relevant national institutions, and by building on existing international and regional human rights mechanisms.
Monitoring progress in the implementation of the Agenda at the local, national, regional and international levels, to disclose inequality and discrimination in this regard through	innovative approaches to data-collection and partnerships with rights-holders, vulnerable and marginalized groups for participatory and inclusive monitoring, and by identifying obstacles as well as actions for accelerated progress.
Engaging with, and holding governments to account for poor or uneven progress in the implementation of the Agenda by	taking implementation progress and obstacles into consideration when reporting to parliaments, the general public and national, regional and international mechanisms.
Protecting the rights of citizens by	responding to, conducting inquiries into, and investigating allegations of rights violations in the context of development and SDG implementation, including in relation to discrimination and inequality that can erode the trust between the State and the people.
Facilitating access to justice, redress and remedy for those who experience abuse and violation of their rights in the process of development by	receiving and processing complaints (where NHRIs have such functions).

As the table demonstrates, these SDG functions proposed by the Mérida Declaration derive from the general mandate and functions of ombuds institutions.

Ombuds institutions are local actors, who often works closely with representatives of international community (international organizations, donors, diplomatic corps, etc.) present on the ground. Furthermore, they have the opportunity to communicate through various avenues with global and regional human rights bodies, well beyond the control of the executive branch. Given such a unique position, ombuds institutions stand as a double intermediary actor, primarily between citizens and the state, and then between the state and international human rights mechanisms (Glušac 2018b: 59). As an intermediary, they contribute to the domestication of international norms and standards. To that end, they are an important factor in making sure that such a process is locally owned.

Factoring in local ownership

Local ownership is a central concept for both SSG/R and development. It is widely regarded as the bedrock and main precondition for successful SSR (Gordon 2014). The concept of local ownership has its roots in the development circles that emphasized the importance of 'empowering local communities and encouraging local participation' in peacebuilding and democracy promotion (Dursun-Özkanca & Vandemoortele 2012: 150). 'The language of ownership' was first used in OECD-DAC's Development Partnerships in the New Global Context document in May 1995 (Chesterman 2007: 7). The OECD endorsed the significance of promoting local ownership in SSR missions back in 2001 (Dursun-Özkanca 2018).

Relevance of local ownership in academic circles is considered uncontested – often acquiring moral legitimacy and orthodoxy in security and development (Oosterveld & Galand 2012; Qehaja and Prezelj 2017; Shinoda 2008). However, while local ownership is part of the 'contemporary commonsense' of SSR (Donais 2009: 119), it remains unclear specifically who the locals are (Donais 2009; Krogstad 2013; Scheye & Peake 2005) and what constitutes ownership (Martin & Wilson 2008; Mobekk 2010).

Local ownership is based on the premise that 'international interventions can lead to sustainable results only if there is a sufficient degree of local input, participation, and control' (Ejdus 2017: 463). In this study, local ownership is understood as the 'extent' to which local constituencies and elected representatives of the target country exercise ownership over the processes of development and security sector reform. In terms of SSR, the principle of local ownership means that the reform of security policies, institutions, and activities in a given country are designed, managed, and implemented by domestic actors rather than external actors (Nathan 2008: 21). In other words, it is regarded as a nationally led and inclusive process in which national and local authorities and civil society are actively engaged and are able to inform decision-making throughout the SSR process, with the support and input of external actors.

As argued by Gordon, if SSR programs are not locally owned, security sector institutions, processes, and policies will likely be less able to respond to local needs; if they do not respond to local needs, efforts to increase security and the rule of law will be compromised, public trust and confidence in the state and its security institutions will be limited, and institutions and other outputs may be rejected (Gordon 2014: 127).

Being national state authorities with rich experience in applying international standards to the national (local) context, ombuds institutions can help localize SSR and SDG efforts. In the right environment, they could help build trust between international and national actors, liaising between them when the frictions occur, and making sure that all social forces are included in the process, and their needs and interests are duly considered.

Methodological framework

To be able to better understand and critically assess the role of ombuds institutions in realizing SDG 16, this sub-chapter develops a methodological framework. Given the comprehensive nature and complexity of those targets and indicators, and mindful of ombuds institutions' mandate and functions, the framework is conceptualized by linking the: (1) main principles of good (security sector) governance, and (2) mandate and functions of ombuds institutions, including those laid down in the Mérida Declaration (2015) and (3) SDG 16 targets.

In this research, the matrix is used to enlist all SDG 16 targets together with corresponding principle(s) of good governance and the indication of the mandate and functions of ombuds institutions through which they can support the realization of individual targets. The central assumption is that ombuds institutions can contribute to achieving all SDG 16 targets. However, the key argument of this study is that their main role should be to support and contribute, not to lead.

Leaving no one behind is a central *credo* of the 2030 Agenda, as well as SSG/R. It is highly relevant for SDG 16. Where do people face disadvantages due to ineffective, unjust, unaccountable, or unresponsive national authorities? Who is affected by inequitable, inadequate, or unjust laws, policies, processes, or budgets? Who is less able or unable to gain influence or participate meaningfully in the decisions that impact them? These questions are at the very heart of SDG 16, which stresses the need for strong institutions that are built on respect for human rights, effective rule of law, and good governance at all levels. With its unique design and place within the overall governance structure, ombuds institutions are themselves human rights, rule of law, and good governance institutions, which may actively influence other public authorities to prioritize respecting the highest human rights standards and the principles of good governance. Furthermore, it is expected that when they encounter maladministration, the most vulnerable citizens would use remedial and accountability mechanisms less frequently than those with more privileged status, due to the lack of knowledge, trust, and resources. Designed as a free, visible, and accessible oversight mechanism, ombuds institutions are perfectly placed to help those disadvantaged and to make public administration accountable for their actions.

In line with that, this study divides the potential contribution of ombuds institutions to the realization of SDG 16 into two main categories (Table 9). The first category, entitled 'leaving no one behind,' focuses on all those who endure disadvantages or deprivations that limit their choices and opportunities relative to others in society. It thus concentrates on the targets to which ombuds institutions actively and directly contribute. These primarily relate to human rights, anti-discrimination, access to justice, reducing violence, and similar. The second category, called 'leaving no one unaccountable,' refers to those targets to whose realization ombuds institutions can contribute indirectly, through their oversight function and through making sure that competent authorities and officials are accountable for their actions.

As the table shows, both categories have six targets allocated. This division is neither surgical nor mathematical, but a useful way to organize the research. It is acknowledged that from the ombuds' perspective, activities falling under 'leaving no one behind' may relatively easily transfer to 'leaving no one unaccountable,' and a little bit harder the other way around. For instance, as it will be shown in the next chapter, ombuds institutions may actively contribute to creating the procedures that would guarantee that all citizens have a legal identity, including birth registration (Target 16.9). This target is placed under 'leaving no one behind.' However, once the proper procedure is established, ombuds institutions may act as an accountability mechanism to make sure that such a procedure is respected in practice.

Furthermore, there is a potential of positive spillover effect of the ombuds' engagement with SDG 16 target, that is, that contributions of ombuds institutions to one target may also have a positive effect on another. For instance, protection of whistleblowers (16.5) can also have positive consequences for the accountability of an institution (16.6), and access to information (16.10).

Table 9: The framework.

Target	Principle	Ombuds' mandate and functions
LEAVING NO ONE BEHIND		
16.1 Significantly reduce all forms of violence and related death rates everywhere	rule of law	monitoring investigating mediation
16.2 End abuse, exploitation, trafficking, and all forms of violence against and torture of children	rule of law	monitoring NPM mandate public outreach and advocacy
16.8 Broaden and strengthen the participation of developing countries in the institutions of global governance	participation responsiveness	advising public outreach and advocacy
16.9 By 2030, provide legal identity for all, including birth registration	rule of law	individual complaint handling mediation legislative advice training
16.10 Ensure public access to information and protect fundamental freedoms, in accordance with national legislation and international agreements	rule of law transparency	all functions
16A Strengthen relevant national institutions, including through international cooperation, for building capacity at all levels, in particular in developing countries, to prevent violence and combat terrorism and crime	rule of law	the existence of A-status NHRI is a key indicator
LEAVING NO ONE UNACCOUNTABLE		
16.3 Promote the rule of law at the national and international levels and ensure equal access to justice for all	rule of law	all functions
16.4 By 2030, significantly reduce illicit financial and arms flows, strengthen the recovery and return of stolen assets and combat all forms of organized crime	rule of law	complaint-handling anti-corruption mandate
16.5 Substantially reduce corruption and bribery in all their forms	accountability	advising education public outreach and advocacy anti-corruption mandate
16.6 Develop effective, accountable, and transparent institutions at all levels	accountability transparency effectiveness	all functions
16.7 Ensure responsive, inclusive, participatory, and representative decision-making at all levels	participation responsiveness	monitoring advising public outreach and advocacy
16B Promote and enforce non-discriminatory laws and policies for sustainable development	participation responsiveness rule of law	legislative advice education public outreach and advocacy investigating complaint-handling

In the next two chapters, this framework is applied empirically. The chapters start with providing more details on the logic and background of 'leaving no one behind' (Chapter 4) and 'leaving no one unaccountable' (Chapter 5), respectively. The chapters then go target by target showing the potential role of ombuds institutions in achieving them. A variety of examples from comparative practice is used to illustrate (1) how ombuds institutions have contributed to achieving those individual goals, and/or (2) what they can do but are yet to start doing.

It should be noted that few ombuds institutions have formally integrated the 2030 Agenda into their work. Thus, many activities (presented in the next two chapters) through which ombuds institutions actively contribute to the realization of the SDGs are neither recognized, nor labeled, as SDG activities by these institutions, but may indeed be viewed as such from an analytical perspective.

CHAPTER 4

Leaving No One Behind

As we embark on this great collective journey, we pledge that no one will be left behind. Recognizing that the dignity of the human person is fundamental, we wish to see the goals and targets met for all nations and peoples and for all segments of society. And we will endeavor to reach the furthest behind first.

—Paragraph 4 in the 2030 Agenda

The implementation of this pledge calls for a comprehensive approach, going well beyond single-factor metrics to understand the severity, multiplicity, and distribution of disadvantages within their societies (UNDP 2018: 8). Inequalities in the context of the SDGs do not refer only to the income-poor, nor do they exist separate from each other. All those living in extreme poverty should be considered left behind, as can those who endure disadvantages or deprivations that limit their choices and opportunities relative to others in society. In other words, people get left behind when they lack the choices and opportunities to participate in and benefit from development progress (UNDP 2018: 3). The ultimate success of the SDGs is directly dependent on political will, which may be lacking where elites defend vested interests. Limited and shrinking space for civil society may also constrain efforts to change minds, reach those who are left behind, and ensure meaningful participation (UNDP 2018: 4).

Equality is at the very center of the 'leaving no one behind' concept. Equality is also fundamental to international human rights. In the human rights framework, equality has instrumental value – inequalities adversely impact the enjoyment of a full array of civil, political, social, economic, and cultural rights. But equality also has intrinsic value – equality in dignity and rights (MacNaughton 2017). As Sakiko Fukuda-Parr (2015) stated, the human rights principles of 'equality and nondiscrimination anchor an alternative framework for analysis of inequality, one that is based on the intrinsic value of equality as a social norm, and one that explores unjust institutions as the source of inequality.'

How to cite this book chapter:
Glušac, L. 2023. *Leaving No One Behind, Leaving No One Unaccountable: Ombuds Institutions, Good (Security Sector) Governance and Sustainable Development Goal 16.* Pp. 37–50. London: Ubiquity Press. DOI: https://doi.org/10.5334/bcw.d. License: CC BY-NC 4.0

Practically, the pledge means all governments must chart a new course aimed specifically at curbing inequalities between people, groups, and places; correcting for legacies of discrimination and exclusion both between and within countries; and prioritizing and fast-tracking progress among the furthest behind (UNDP 2018: 8). However, such prioritization must not be only rhetorical. As noted by Winkler and Satterthwaite (2017: 1076), the litmus test for whether the SDGs will truly 'leave no one behind' is not whether the SDG goals and targets include such (aspirational) language, but whether this language will translate into the implementation of the goals through policies, programs, and specific measures to eliminate discrimination and advance progress for marginalized groups.

Given the urgency of achieving the SDGs, countries have to adopt integrated approaches that would allow working on the several goals simultaneously. UNDP has presented the most elaborate account of the 'leaving no one behind' approach, advocating for integrated approaches which simultaneously: (1) improve what is known about who is left behind, where they are, and why; (2) empower marginalized populations to act and claim their rights; and (3) build the capacity of governments to adopt equity-focused and rights-based SDG targets, policies, and budgets which are inclusive and accountable (UNDP 2018: 21). Ombuds institutions may contribute to all three 'levers.'

To improve what is known about who is left behind and where essentially means to examine why people are left behind. Countries must thus collect and use more and better disaggregated data and people-driven information. Ombuds institutions are already recognized as important data providers for the SDGs (DIHR 2019, 2020).

Empowering marginalized populations means motivating and capacitating them to act and claim their rights. As premier human rights complaint-handling mechanisms, ombuds institutions are natural candidates to support this effort. With their broad mandate, they are well suited to protect people who may experience multiple discrimination (on the basis of gender, indigeneity, minority status, age, disability, and similar).

Empowering those who are left behind, however, means much more than only protecting the rights of marginalized populations. It also means 'ensuring their meaningful participation in decision making and establishing safe and inclusive mechanisms for their civic engagement' (UNDP 2018: 24). In other words, building trust in government institutions, including independent authorities, such as ombuds institutions, is a vital precondition for the readiness of marginalized populations to engage with them and to recognize them as the authority that could protect their rights. UNDP (2018: 24) has explicitly recognized that NHRIs 'play a vital role in bridging state and stakeholder efforts to include excluded and marginalized groups and advance non-discrimination and equity in national policy making.'

Building the capacity of governments to adopt equity-focused and rights-based SDG targets, policies, and budgets refers to the ability to enact policies, laws, reforms, and interventions to confront the drivers that leave people behind across different SDGs. These should all ultimately lead to improving public services on national, regional, and local levels. As shown in Chapter 2, ombuds institutions are designed to do exactly this: to ensure the provision of citizen-orientated public services.

Although the SDGs were negotiated and adopted under the spotlights of the world's capitals, their practical implementation must reach even the smallest communities around the globe; otherwise, they are not as global or universal as they aspire to be. A parallel with human rights is rewarding here. Eleanor Roosevelt (1958), who chaired the Universal Declaration of Human Rights Committee, famously said that 'universal human rights begin in small places, close to home; so close and so small that they cannot be seen on any map of the world.' The same applies to development, that is, the SDGs, which must reach every inch of the world to be truly global. Both development and human rights call for the symbiotic endeavor of national and local actors, instead of becoming arenas of contestation between local and national authorities (Glušac 2018a).

It is those who are isolated, either due to geography or other factors, that are most vulnerable. In today's world characterized by the omnipresence of technology, the inability to access mobile phones and other internet-enabled devices prevents many of the poorest and most marginalized people from fully participating in their country's economy, society, and political system. As of 2021, the International Telecommunication Union (ITU) estimates that approximately 4.9 billion people – or 63 percent of the world's population – have access to the internet. Although this represents an increase of 17 percent since 2019, with 782 million people estimated to have come online during that period, this still leaves 2.9 billion people offline (ITU n.d.). People in developing countries are particularly disadvantaged as, because of the 2.9 billion still offline, an estimated 96 percent live in those countries (ITU 2021). Furthermore, globally, people in urban areas are twice as likely to use the internet as those in rural areas (76 percent urban compared to 39 percent rural). In the least developed countries (LDCs), urban dwellers are almost four times as likely to use the internet as people living in rural areas (47 percent urban compared to 13 percent rural), according to the 2021 data gathered by ITU (2021). In increasingly interconnected societies and technology-enabled economies, digital exclusion translates into exclusion on many fronts from economic opportunities to participate in 'the public sphere' (UN Broadband Commission 2017).

The COVID-19 pandemic only reiterated the importance of internet access, as many public services were forced to cancel in-person access to their offices. To mitigate this, many public offices, including ombuds institutions, invested efforts to become more accessible through online services. Indeed, the digitalization of complaints-lodging procedures and case-management systems was the key development in the work of most ombuds institutions during the first wave of COVID-19 (Glušac & Kuduzovic 2021: 2).

According to the survey conducted by DCAF in the summer of 2020, which included responses from 41 ombuds institutions in 37 countries coming from five continents, the pandemic accelerated processes of digitalization and has created an impetus for more flexible working environments (Glušac & Kuduzovic 2021: 8). The need for greater adaptability and increased remote access to ombuds institutions has thus been an opportunity to modernize the workstreams of ombuds offices, instituting and refining complaints mechanisms that are accessible through social media or smartphone apps in some cases (Glušac & Kuduzovic 2021: 9).

Being accessible to citizens through various channels is of great importance for ombuds institutions as grievance and complaint mechanisms (Dahlvik 2022). Outside of the traditional means of lodging complaints, in-person or by mail, many ombuds institutions worldwide also introduced the option to file complaints by email or by using special forms on their institutional websites. In addition, some ombuds institutions have tested ways to receive complaints via their social media channels, while others have also used popular instant messaging applications to communicate with citizens (e.g., Senegal and Côte d'Ivoire). According to DCAF's survey, 51 percent of ombuds institutions have introduced new digital procedures from the start of the COVID-19 pandemic, to enable citizens to file complaints by email, web form, or social media (Glušac & Kuduzovic 2021: 12).

Speaking on the challenges to the work of ombuds institutions posed by COVID-19, the Ombudsperson for Bermuda and President of the Caribbean and Latin America Region of International Ombudsman Institute (IOI), Victoria Pearman (2020), has encouraged her peers to use both traditional and electronic means of communication, to remain visible and accessible to the citizens without reliable internet connections, particularly in rural areas, who still mostly rely on landline phones. Automatic phone readings have been widely used by ombuds institutions (during the times when the offices were closed) to transmit important service information and provide assurances to citizens that their messages were regularly checked by ombuds staff.

The isolation that leads to exclusion goes beyond access to the internet or phone network. People are left behind and left open to vulnerability and inequality when they are deprived of access to justice, equal protection under the law, and basic services, such as roads, public transport, sanitation, and energy, etc. As argued by UNDP (2018: 19), 'the more severe the poverty and inequities people experience, the more tightly interwoven and enduring such barriers become and the more vulnerable people become to exploitation and human rights abuses.'

What follows is an attempt to explore what ombuds institutions could and should do to contribute to achieving six targets that directly relate to preventing exploitation and human rights abuses.

Reducing all forms of violence (16.1)

People are left behind when they are vulnerable to risks related to violence, conflict, or displacement. The impact of violent conflict can cause entire communities, regions or countries to be left behind, and they can also often spill over national borders (UNDP 2018: 19). Here, violence is defined as 'the intentional use of physical force or power, threatened or actual, against oneself, another person, or against a group or community, that either result in or has a high likelihood of resulting in injury, death, psychological harm, maldevelopment, or deprivation' (WHO 2002).

Extreme poverty is increasingly concentrated among vulnerable groups displaced by violent conflict and within countries and regions affected by conflict (World Bank 2016). In 2020, fragile contexts and conflict-affected settings were home to 23 percent of the world's population and 76.5 percent of those living in extreme poverty globally (OECD 2020). Violence, armed conflict, and forced displacement are concentrated in fragile countries and territories. In 2019, 79 percent of deaths from violent conflict and 96 percent of deaths from state-based armed conflict occurred in fragile countries and territories. Fragility, multidimensional poverty, and inequalities mutually reinforce each other, as fragility and conflict can lead to the absence of public services, intolerance, and limited access to resources, which in turn can provoke grievances resulting in mistrust and conflict (UNDP 2018: 17). According to the OECD (2020), fragility is the combination of exposure to risk and insufficient coping capacity of the state, systems, and/or communities to manage, absorb, or mitigate those risks. Fragility can lead to negative outcomes including violence, poverty, inequality, displacement, and environmental and political degradation. In 2020, 57 countries and territories were defined as fragile contexts by OECD.

Ombuds institutions may serve as early-warning systems for violent conflict and tools for preventing such conflicts. By quickly responding to and rectifying grievances, ombuds institutions address one of the main root causes of violent conflict. Working with security and judicial actors is essential in this regard, both when discussing armed conflict and peacetime violence, such as intentional homicides or other forms of physical, psychological, or sexual violence, which are all recognized through SDG 16 indicators.

Through media reports and by addressing individual or collective complaints, ombuds institutions may learn of systemic problems within the communities which may potentially lead to conflict. Ombuds institutions must be present on the ground to be able to recognize such developments and engage with local communities and stakeholders timely. This particularly applies to multiethnic and multireligious societies, with a history of conflict. For instance, in order to foster inter-ethnic relations in Serbia, the Protector of Citizens (Ombudsman) established three local offices in South Serbia's municipalities where Albanians form the majority. This helped build trust in public institutions and provided the local community with direct access to national authority with strong mandates and powers.

Ombuds institutions are well-placed to develop trainings for security actors on working in multiethnic and multireligious environments. Learning about the similarities and differences of various social groups populating the country is a precondition to making them feel like equal and productive members of the society.

Mediation and offering good services are two rewarding avenues for working with local community leaders and national actors to resolve conflicts in the early stages or in post-conflict settings, especially when security forces (military and/or armed police) are deployed on the ground. Being independent and impartial, ombuds institutions should work on building stronger ties and confidence with local communities, to be able to bring different social forces to the table and foster dialogue. For example, ombuds institutions from Ecuador (environmental rights), Colombia (peace negotiations), and Costa Rica (public protests) have served as initiators and/or conveners of multi-stakeholder dialogues meant to bring closer the positions of different social actors.

Beyond armed conflict, by working with local administrations, social services, and the police, ombuds institutions may contribute to suppressing family and gender-based violence. Responding quickly to any information received or learned may save lives and protect those most vulnerable.

A good example of an NHRI's systemic action aimed at combating all forms of violence, including sexual harassment, is the Australian Human Rights Commission, which conducted a national survey to investigate the prevalence, nature, and reporting of sexual harassment in Australian workplaces and the community more broadly. The 2018 survey was conducted both online and by telephone with a sample of over 10,000 Australians. It revealed that one in three people (33 percent) have experienced sexual harassment at work in the last five years. In response to the survey, Australia's Sex Discrimination Commissioner announced an unprecedented National Inquiry into sexual harassment (DIHR 2019: 20).

Ending abuse, exploitation, trafficking, and all forms of violence against and torture of children (16.2)

No violence against children is justifiable and all violence against children is preventable
—Paulo Sérgio Pinheiro (2006: 3)

This target is of great importance for general ombuds institutions and those ombuds institutions focusing on children's rights, which exist in a number of countries. Those specialized children ombuds institutions often exist in parallel with general ombuds institutions. That is the case in, for instance, Croatia, Cyprus, Finland, Ireland, Lithuania, or Slovakia. However, more frequently, the protection and promotion of the rights of the child are delegated to general ombuds institutions, which often establish special departments for the rights of the child. Furthermore, many countries appoint a Deputy Ombudsperson for Children within the general ombuds institution to emphasize the importance of protecting the youngest members of society. This is the case in, for example, Serbia, Greece, North Macedonia, Montenegro, Romania, and Slovenia. Finally, in some countries, as in the Netherlands, the Ombudsperson for Children is part of the National Ombudsman but operates as an independent institution.

Although at first sight this target may seem less relevant for specialized military ombuds institutions, it actually may be of high importance, especially in the context of peace operations. While peacekeepers are instrumental in assisting communities in volatile regions and promoting a brighter future after conflicts, there have unfortunately been instances where some peacekeepers have taken advantage of the very people they were sent to protect. These instances include (but are not limited to) UN peacekeeping operations in the Democratic Republic of the Congo (United Nations Organization Mission in the Democratic Republic of the Congo – MONUC and United Nations Organization Stabilization Mission in the Democratic Republic of the Congo – MONUSCO), Central African Republic (United Nations Multidimensional Integrated Stabilization Mission in the Central African Republic – MINUSCA), and Haiti (United Nations Stabilization Mission in Haiti – MINUSTAH), where acts such as rape and other forms of sexual exploitation and abuse, including against children, have been reported and documented (Nordås & Rustad 2013; Kovatch 2016; Lee & Bartels 2020).

Recognizing the gravity of these incidents and to ensure accountability, the United Nations has established various channels for investigating allegations and holding individuals responsible. These include internal investigations, collaboration with national authorities, and dedicated units within peacekeeping missions specifically focused on preventing and addressing sexual exploitation and abuse. One of the potential national remedial mechanisms in these situations could be ombuds institutions. In the framework of the annual International Conference of Ombuds Institutions for the Armed Forces (ICOAF), ombuds institutions have already recognized the potential to be more actively involved in peace operations, in order to protect the rights of both armed forces personnel deployed abroad and the local population. They have also noted a complex environment pertinent to peace operations, such as post-conflict fragile contexts, the involvement of multiple jurisdictions, and different mandates of ombuds institutions (ICOAF 2016). The Dutch National Ombudsman (and Dutch Inspector-General), the German Parliamentary Commissioner for the Armed Forces, and the Parliamentary Ombud's Committee for the Norwegian Armed Forces have been forerunners in this regard, conducting separate or joint field visits to the troops in Mali (2016, UN mission), Norway (2022, NATO military exercise), and Lithuania (2023, joint troops stationed there). The ombuds work in this area is still very much in progress, with tangible results yet to be seen, particularly in terms of protecting the rights of local population, including children. Various challenges are observed, most notably, legal and institutional quagmire on the line: mission headquarters – mission command – national contingent command – national headquarters. All these instances have some kind of complaint mechanisms that are extremely difficult to map, let alone comprehend and use. Ombuds institutions have to learn how to navigate through these waters, making sure to cooperate well with their counterparts in the country of deployment, and to be visible and accessible to potential complainants on the ground. The latter has proven to be a challenging task even in their own backyards. Still, it is commendable that ombuds institutions are committed to this goal and invest considerable efforts to achieve it.

Whilst it is expected that jurisdictional issues count in an international environment, this should be avoided on the national level. Whatever the institutional setup, the legal framework must provide for a clear division of mandates and powers of different public authorities, to avoid conflicts of positive or negative jurisdiction, and to maximize the protection of the rights of the child. Globally, much more effort is needed to suppress violence against children. According to the latest UN data, violence against children is widespread, affecting children regardless of wealth or social status. In 76 (mostly low- and middle-income) countries with available data from 2013 to 2021, 8 in 10 children aged one to 14 years of age were subjected to some form of psychological aggression and/or physical punishment at home in the previous month (UN 2022: para. 152).

Monitoring is the key function of ombuds institutions through which they can contribute to achieving this target. In this context, monitoring 'does not consist merely of passive observation, but rather calls for proactively seeking information, ensuring that it is accurate and then using it to redress wrongs, halt violations and prevent abuse' (UNICEF 2020: 7).

Preventive and reactive visits to all places where children are cared for or detained without the possibility to leave freely (usually based on a judicial or administrative order) should be the highest priority. The main settings are those in which children are in institutional or residential care or are deprived of liberty (e.g., juvenile detention centers or other facilities managed by the juvenile justice system). They may also include prison-type facilities; detention centers hosting children and their parent(s); hospitals and psychiatric institutions; education or rehabilitation centers; and asylum centers, refugee camps, or reception facilities for children on the move, whether unaccompanied or with their parent(s) (UNICEF 2020).

Handling individual complaints from children or regarding children should be a daily priority of ombuds institutions. However, when discussing the prevention of violence against children, more systemic efforts are needed to achieve this complex SDG target. Drafting thematic reports may be regarded as a particularly rewarding avenue of potentially high impact on realizing 16.2. Conducting in-depth studies on the aspects that connect the rights of the child with SDGs may also be another option. Child trafficking and child beggary are among the topics that connect the two in the most comprehensive manner.

Prevention of child trafficking and child beggary requires a strategic engagement of different law enforcement and intelligence/security agencies. Both often constitute organized crime, with transnational elements. Children victims of these crimes are de facto deprived of their liberty, with little or no real possibility to report or complain to either police or human rights mechanisms. Thus, ombuds institutions should be vigilant in monitoring the developments in this area and keep regular consultations with police and social welfare centers to contribute to suppressing these crimes.

The principle of participation – listening to the child's opinion regarding the matters of his/her concern and paying due attention to that opinion – is one of the basic principles enshrined in the UN Convention on the Rights of the Child. Including children in its work should also be a strategy of ombuds institutions. This is sometimes done through the establishment of special permanent bodies, such as the Young Advisors Panel or similar structure. This has been done on both national (e.g., Greece, Serbia, Ireland) and international levels (e.g., the European Network of Young Advisors – ENYA – a child/young people participatory project supported by the members of the European Network of Ombudspersons for Children – ENOC). Such young advisory panels secure a permanent form of participation of children and youth in the activities of ombuds institutions. They usually consist of a limited number of young advisors (up to 30), aged up to 18, elected periodically among pupils that have responded to a public call. The main role of such panels is to convey to ombuds institutions the topics that are important to children and young people, point out the problems they face, present their views, and raise issues that are important to improving the position of children and youth in a given country. For example, the Young Advisors Panel of the Protector of Citizens (Ombudsman) of Serbia has taken active participation in drafting the Child Protection Policy of the Protector of Citizens, aimed at prevention and timely and adequate response to all types of violence against children (Protector of Citizens 2021). This has helped the Protector of Citizens to better understand constantly developing manifestations of violence against children, including peer violence, particularly in cyberspace, which is an increasingly present phenomenon. As a result, the Protector of Citizens is better equipped to oversee the work of police, when it comes to the cases of violence against children.

Broadening and strengthening the participation of developing countries in the institutions of global governance (16.8)

This SDG 16 target aims at providing for more inclusive and active participation of developing countries in institutions of global governance. There is only one indicator associated with it: the proportion of members and voting rights of developing countries in international organizations. It does not include any tangible goal in terms of the percentage or similar measure.

It is challenging to define 'developing countries' in the context of this indicator, as there is no current definition of developing and developed countries (or areas) within the UN system. In 1996, the distinction between 'developed regions' and 'developing regions' was introduced to the standard country or area codes for statistical use (known as M49). However, after the adoption of the SDGs and following consultation with other international and supranational organizations active in official statistics, the United Nations removed 'developed regions' and 'developing regions' from the M49 in December 2021 (UN Statistics n.d.).

At first sight, this target does not seem to have much in common with ombuds institutions. Nonetheless, this target could be applied to ombuds institutions, in terms of the proportion of ombuds institutions and other forms of NHRIs coming from developing countries in the governing bodies of two global peer institutions – GANHRI and IOI. Being present in these structures helps ombuds institutions from developing countries to influence the strategic priorities of these peer networks, by promoting the topics which would not otherwise be on their agenda. This may then lead to stronger advocacy in global arena, as GANHRI and IOI regularly engage with key stakeholders, including the United Nations and the Council of Europe.

It should be noted that neither GANHRI nor IOI have a policy on including a certain number of developing countries in their governing structures.[1] Still, both organizations have put strong emphasis on equal regional representation.

---

[1] The author thanks a reviewer for raising this question.

To ensure a fair balance of regional representation, GANHRI recognizes four regional networks (Africa, Americas, Asia-Pacific, and Europe). Each regional network appoints four members and one alternate member accredited with 'A' status to represent the regional network on the GANHRI Bureau, as the main governing body, for a three-year term. Only NHRIs accredited with 'A' status are eligible to be voting members of GANHRI. This applies to both General Assembly and the Bureau. For the current composition of the GANHRI Bureau (2023), see Table 10.

Table 10: Composition of the GANHRI Bureau (2023).

Region/Countries				
Africa	Morocco	Zimbabwe	Ghana	DR Congo
Americas	Bolivia	Canada	Guatemala	Argentina
Asia-Pacific	Qatar	Australia	Jordan	Korea
Europe	Finland	Bulgaria	Norway	Albania

Countries highlighted green in the table are considered developing countries by the World Bank's list of low- and middle-income countries, that concentrates on gross national income per capita (GNI) and the UN Human Development Index (HDI) considering a broad range of factors, including economic growth, life expectancy, health, education, and quality of life. Those in blue are considered developing countries by the World Bank, but not by HDI. The opposite cases would be in yellow, but there are none. Looking at the table, it could be said that developing countries are well-represented in the GANHRI Bureau.

The IOI, established in 1978, is the only global organization for the cooperation of more than 200 ombuds institutions from more than 100 countries worldwide. In contrast to GANHRI, which gathers only institutions operating on the national level, the IOI also includes regional and local ombuds institutions. The IOI is organized into six regional chapters (Africa, Asia, Australasia & Pacific, Europe, the Caribbean & Latin America, and North America). It is governed by the Board of Directors, which consists of the members of all regions, elected for a four-year period. The voting members of each region elect their representatives to the Board of Directors, depending on the number of the voting members: a maximum of 3 regional directors where there are fewer than 20 voting members; a maximum of 4 regional directors where there are 20 or more voting members; and a maximum of 5 regional directors where there are 60 or more voting members. The voting members of each region then elect a Regional President (RP) from amongst the elected regional directors.

Given the current number of the voting members, the composition of the IOI Board of Directors is as follows in Table 11:

Table 11: Composition of the IOI Board of Directors (IOI 2023).

Region	Regional President	Regional Director	Regional Director	Regional Director	Regional Director
Africa	Kenya	Angola	South Africa	Zambia	
Asia	Thailand	South Korea	Pakistan	Pakistan	
Australasia & Pacific	Australia	New Zealand	Australia		
Europe	Greece	Portugal	United Kingdom	Belgium	Slovenia
Caribbean & Latin America	Mexico	Curacao	Sint Maarten	Argentina	
North America	Canada	USA	Canada		

Note: The same color scheme is used as in the previous table.

As the candidates for the Board of Directors are elected individually, it is possible to have more than one director from the same country, as in the case of Australia and Canada. In addition, as the IOI accepts regional and local ombuds institutions, it recognizes Curaçao and Sint Maarten, despite the fact they are constituent parts of the Kingdom of the Netherlands. In sum, around half of the members of the IOI Board come from developing countries, expectedly from Africa and Asia regions, which is a solid result.

Providing legal identity for all, including birth registration (16.9)

Legal identity has a critical role to ensure the global community upholds its promise of leaving no one behind as espoused in the 2030 Agenda. Legal identity is widely acknowledged to be catalytic for achieving at least ten of the SDGs, as data generated from civil registration and population registers support the measurement of over 60 SDG indicators (United Nations Legal Identity Expert Group 2019: 2).

This SDG target holds great promise – to implement the fundamental right of everyone to be recognized as a person before the law. Enshrined in Article 6 of the Universal Declaration on Human Rights and Article 16 of the International Covenant on Civil and Political Rights, this fundamental right to a legal identity is a prerequisite for exercising all other rights.

By providing all children with proof of legal identity from day one, their rights can be protected and universal access to justice and social services can be enabled. Yet, according to the latest data, the births of around 1 in 4 children under age 5 worldwide today have never been officially recorded based on data for 2012–2021; only half of the children under five in sub-Saharan Africa have had their births registered (UN 2022: para. 159). This problem goes well beyond birth registration, as it refers to many people worldwide without any personal documents, making them 'legally invisible.' When people are unable to prove their identity, they cannot access basic services like education and health care. In such situations, they turn to informal networks in order to substitute for formal services. They become more exposed to fraud, human trafficking, and other crimes. At the same time, due to their status, access to law enforcement and justice systems is quite limited. To make the situation even worse, sometimes they actively avoid going to police or any other public institutions, as they can be subjected to criminal or misdemeanor proceedings, because in many countries having no personal documents is illegal. Hence, the phenomenon of crime underreporting is very much present among this population. It is in the interest of the state authorities to resolve this problem and make sure that all citizens are legally recognized.

Despite great potential for the promotion of individual rights associated with a legal identity, registration and identification systems may also serve to suppress and exclude, being a tool of state control and surveillance.

As shown by Lyon (2010: 607) and Ajana (2013), governments have regarded the expansion of registration and identification systems as a useful tool for border and movement controls and counter-terrorism, but also suppression of opposition in more authoritarian regimes. Hence, civil society organizations such as Access Now or Privacy International have scrutinized the potential for abuse of identification systems and advocated for robust data protection legislation and privacy safeguards (Beduschi 2019). As argued by Sperfeldt (2021: 8), 'this [security] perspective is usually absent from official documents and advertising materials surrounding the SDGs, but nevertheless an important consideration for governments seeking to implement universal identification and registration systems.' Another problem is that there is no universally accepted definition of legal identity.

As premier independent human rights authorities, (general) ombuds institutions are well-placed to actively contribute to achieving this target, particularly in the contexts where the right to legal identity and the procedure of providing the proof of legal identity are not legally or procedurally fully regulated. Special attention should be given to ensure that identification and registration systems are introduced with the purpose of inclusion, not the exclusion of stateless people or those with no personal documents. The case of the Serbian Ombudsman (Protector of Citizens) is a good illustration of how this can be done in practice.

In 2010, the Protector of Citizens (then Saša Janković) identified the problem of the "so-called legally invisible citizens, that is persons who have not been entered into birth or other registers (mostly internally displaced persons from Kosovo and Metohija, namely the Roma), thereby being unable to exercise their civil rights." (Protector of Citizens 2011: 25). The Protector of Citizens conducted several control procedures which resulted in registration in the register (of births, deaths, and marriages) and issuance of personal documents for these persons. However, the systemic problem remained. In 2012, the Ombudsman published a comprehensive 'Report on the Status of "Legally Invisible" Persons in the Republic of Serbia' (Protector of Citizens 2012). The same year, the Ombudsman initiated amendments to the Law on Non-Contentious Procedure, which passage enabled persons who were not able to register in birth registers in the administrative procedure of late registration of birth, to exercise this right within a reasonable time through judicial proceedings. Before the Ministry of the Interior, the Protector of Citizens also initiated amendments to the Law on Permanent and Temporary Residence of Citizens and the Law on Identity Cards, which was passed by the National Assembly, whereby citizens who had not been able to exercise their rights because they did not have a registered permanent residence were enabled to do so after registering at the address of the social work center in the local self-government in which they lived (Protector of Citizens 2013: 63). To assist the authorities in implementing this new system, the Protector of Citizens, the Ministry of Justice and Public Administration, and the United Nations High Commissioner for Refugees concluded the Memorandum of Understanding (MoU). Under this MoU, the Protector of Citizens has continued to oversee the implementation of the new legislation and has participated in several rounds of trainings for judges, registrars, employees of centers for social work, and Roma organizations on how to implement the new procedures in practice.

Ensuring public access to information and protecting fundamental freedoms (16.10)

Judging by its title, one would rightly assume that this SDG 16 target is among the broadest defined targets in the entire 2030 Agenda. However, when analyzed through the lenses of the indicators, the perspective changes. There are only two indicators associated with this target: (1) the number of verified cases of killing, kidnapping, enforced disappearance, arbitrary detention, and torture of journalists, associated media personnel, trade unionists, and human rights advocates in the previous 12 months; and (2) the number of countries that adopt and implement constitutional, statutory, and/or policy guarantees for public access to information. The former relates to 'protecting fundamental freedoms' and has a narrow focus on the physical well-being of the media and civil society representatives, while the latter concentrates on 'ensuring public access to information.' These indicators do not necessarily reflect the stated aim of the target itself, nor they can objectively testify if the target is achieved or not. Still, this is what the states have agreed upon.

Ombuds institutions and the media are both oversight mechanisms. Before the widespread development of independent oversight institutions, it was the media that was often described as the fourth branch of power. The media is of crucial importance for the ultimate success of ombuds' efforts. It serves as a megaphone of the findings of ombuds institutions and a pressuring channel. Often public officials react to ombuds' requests and recommendations only after being pressured by media reports. Cooperation with media outlets (traditional and electronic) is essential for ombuds institutions' ability to conduct large-scale advocacy, awareness-raising, and educational campaigns.

An excellent example of the cooperation between an ombuds institution and public media is found in Austria. Since 1979 (with a hiatus between 1991 and 2002), the Austrian Ombudsman

Board (AOB) has a weekly broadcast on public TV (*Bürgeranwalt*) in which recent cases are discussed in the presence of an ombudsperson, a complainant, and sometimes representatives of the relevant authority (Dahlvik and Pohn-Weidinger 2021). Through this show, the ombuds institution is provided with the opportunity to present its work, elaborate on its mandate and approach, and demonstrate the power to find solutions not only for individual problems of citizens but also to address more systemic issues. As noted by Dahlvik and Pohn-Weidinger (2021), the broadcast is highly popular, attracting an average of 324,000 viewers in 2017 (a 23 percent market share at that time slot). According to the head of the public broadcasting company, between 2007 and 2018, around 1,000 cases were discussed on the program (Hadler 2018). Such a broadcast remains rather unique in the ombuds world.

Ombuds institutions also regularly follow the media for information-gathering purposes. As argued by one of three ombudspersons of Bosnia and Herzegovina, Ljubinko Mitrović:

> Namely, media reporting on citizens' life situations, their needs and interests is the best way for an Ombudsman to learn about the violations of the rights and fundamental freedoms of citizens. This information in a number of cases serves as the basis for the opening of cases *ex officio* in order to examine the veracity of the allegations presented by the media and to take the appropriate action in accordance with the Ombudsman's mandate aimed at redress and remedy of human rights and fundamental freedoms violations (Mitrović & Romić 2017: 97).

In return, ombuds institutions pay particular attention to protecting the rights of media workers (journalists, editors, etc.), as they are often subject to threats and attacks coming from various sources, including government officials and the criminal milieu.

In many corners of the world, journalists and other human rights defenders are subject to state violence, illegal detention, and even enforced disappearance. This has particularly been the case in Latin America. For instance, the 2021 report by Ecuador's Alliance for Human Rights examines abuses against indigenous and environmental rights defenders over the past 10 years, and finds 449 defenders subjected to intimidation, threats, harassment, persecution, and assassination (AOHR 2021). Since 2019, the Ombudsman of Ecuador has invested efforts to bring public authorities and civil society to the table, by organizing the interinstitutional discussion on formulating a public policy to guarantee the work of human and environmental rights defenders (AOHR 2021).

Ombuds institutions should pay particular attention to human rights defenders who are detained, to make sure that such state actions do not present retaliation or suppression of media freedom, but are indeed legally justified. Ombuds institutions can also use their right to visit them in detention, to make sure they are treated fairly. Independent media should support these efforts by objectively reporting and participating in awareness-raising campaigns.

The media are, however, not always ombuds' friends; sometimes they are foes, as they are used as channels for attacking ombuds institutions. Government-controlled media are sometimes used for smear campaigns against ombuds institutions when their actions are not favorable to those in power (see more in Vladisavljević, Krstić & Pavlovic 2019).

Speaking of access to information, firstly, there is a question of the ability of ombuds institutions to access information to be able to fulfil their mandate. This type of access to information should not be confused with the access to public information or information of public importance, which is the focus of this SDG 16 target.

As discussed in Chapter 2, public authorities must cooperate with the ombuds institution, including by providing it with unhindered access to information (oral and written), premises, and people. Such an exchange of information is usually regulated by the founding law on the ombuds institution or by more general law on the exchange of information between state authorities if such a law exists. The problems with access to information by ombuds institutions indeed exist in practice, particularly with classified information (Glušac 2018b), but that is a separate question.

In other words, the law regulating access to public information should not apply in the case of ombuds institutions. Such a law is meant for the public access to information, that is, by the citizens and the media, most usually. Nevertheless, it would be wrong to conclude that such a law is not relevant for ombuds institutions.

Oversight of the implementation of the law on access to public information is usually delegated to either a new, separate institution, such as the Commissioner for Information of Public Importance (or of a similar title) or to an already existing independent body, not rarely an ombuds institution. In the former case, if the general ombuds institution exists, it is usually in charge of overseeing the work of the Commissioner, as it is part of the public administration. In the latter case, it is the ombuds institution that has an additional mandate, and with that a primary responsibility of making sure that the public is, indeed, able to access information of public importance. This is, for instance, the case in Kenya, where the mandate of the Commission on Administrative Justice (Office of the Ombudsman) is two-fold. As a constitutional commission established under the 2010 Constitution, it tackles maladministration in the public sector. Since 2016, it has also had the mandate of overseeing and enforcing the implementation of the Access to Information Act. In sum, ombuds institutions can assist the public in ensuring their right to access to information and that the laws and policies guaranteeing this right are respected.

Strengthening relevant national institutions (16.A)

The NHRI indicator is a tribute to the sound work which so many NHRIs are doing
—UN High Commissioner for Human Rights (GANHRI 2017: 33)

As mentioned above, besides 10 'regular' targets, SDG 16 includes two targets described as 'means of implementation' (MoI). The first MoI target is this one – strengthening relevant national institutions. The Member States have defined only one indicator of the achievement of this target: the existence of independent national human rights institutions in compliance with the Paris Principles.

Ombuds institutions and other NHRIs can use this indicator to advance their legislation and overall status. The National Human Rights Commission of Mongolia (NHRCM) took part in national consultations on defining national indicators and targets for the SDGs. The NHRCM provided its feedback on this indicator and its comments were included in the national indicators and sources. The NHRCM recommended amending the Law on NHRCM and including specific references to the Paris Principles as indicators. Subsequently, the Law on NHRCM was revised, and the new law was adopted in January 2020 (DIHR 2020: 8), contributing to NHRCM's successful A-status reaccreditation in 2021.

To achieve this target, all UN Member States should have A-status NHRI by 2030. In 2015, the Office of the High Commissioner for Human Rights (OHCHR) prepared a chart showing that in order to reach this indicator by 2030, the Member States must establish 10 new A-status NHRIs per year (Figure 2). This further reiterates the commitment to establish a Paris Principles-compliant institution made by the vast majority of UN Member States under the Universal Periodic Review (UPR) (Glušac 2022).

According to UN data, on average, four new NHRIs applied for accreditation every year for the period 2015–2017 compared to only one new application for NHRI accreditation per year for the period 2018–2021. In sum, in 2022, only 43 percent of countries benefit from independent NHRIs (UN 2022: para. 161).

As can be seen from the table, according to this plan, there should be already 127 A-status NHRIs in 2023. As of April 2023, there are only 88 (GANHRI 2023). Looking ahead, starting from the current 88 NHRIs, to reach the indicator, there should be 16 new A-status NHRIs every year until 2030 (Figure 3).

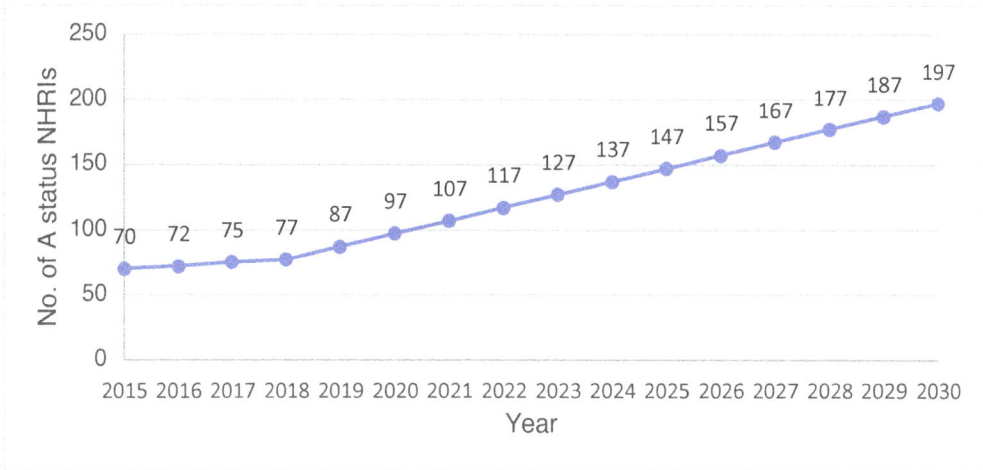

Figure 2: Accelerating the pace of progress of A-status NHRIs per year (2015–2030) (DIHR 2019: 9).

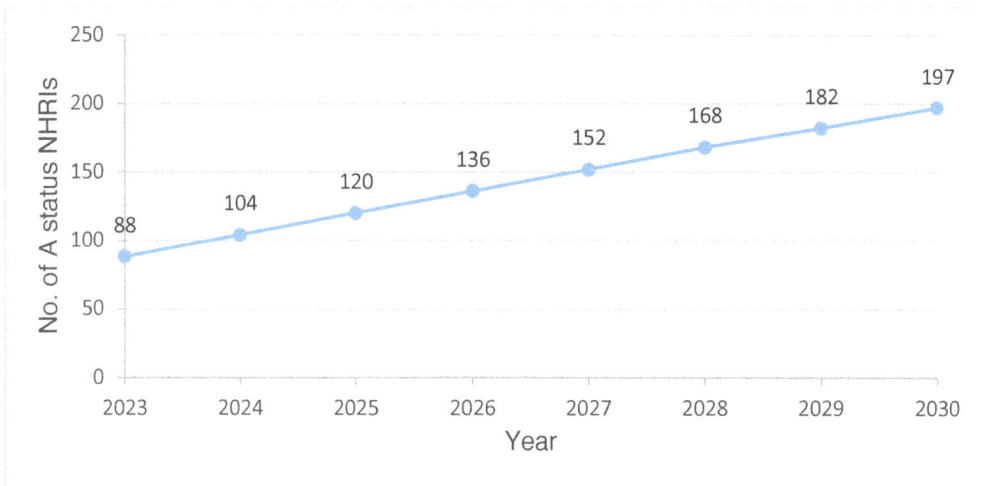

Figure 3: Accelerating the pace of progress of A-status NHRIs per year (2022–2030) (by author).

This would be extremely hard if not impossible to achieve. There are more than a few strong reasons for this. Firstly, judging from the pace since 2015, it is highly unlikely that the Member States would suddenly start adopting complex laws such as those establishing NHRIs at such a speed to allow for this indicator to be reached. Domestic negotiations for the establishment of an NHRI usually take years, particularly in developed countries, such as Norway or Sweden, because they affect an entire national human rights architecture (Glušac 2022). On the other hand, with a visible global trend of democratic backsliding, it is unlikely that such regimes will be interested in creating or strengthening an NHRI.[2] Secondly, even when a new independent human rights institution is established, it cannot immediately apply for A status, because GANHRI's Subcommittee on Accreditation assesses not only the legal framework, but also the practice of an institution (see more in: De Beco and Murray 2015; Langtry and Roberts Lyer 2021). Hence, it takes at least a few years before the institution could apply. Furthermore, applying for an NHRI status does

---

[2] The author thanks the reviewer for bringing up this argument.

not mean that the institution will receive A status. In fact, the Subcommittee has recently downgraded some NHRIs from A to B status (e.g., Sri Lanka, Azerbaijan, and Hungary). Finally, the Subcommittee on Accreditation holds only two sessions per year. At each session, it does not only assess new applications; it also conducts reaccreditations (as each A-status NHRI is reassessed every five years) and often performs deferrals (postponed reaccreditations), alterations of accreditations, and special reviews. As an illustration, at its second session in 2022, the SCA has had the following agenda, seen in Table 12:

Table 12: SCA agenda for the October 2022 session (GANHRI 2022).

Type of procedure	Institutions to be reviewed
(New) Accreditation	Turkey
Reaccreditation	Canada, Colombia, Great Britain, Indonesia, Liberia, Niger, Norway, Perú, Sierra Leone
Deferral	Cyprus, El Salvador, Nepal, Northern Ireland
Alteration of Accreditation	Sri Lanka
Special Review	Madagascar

SCA is comprised of four (representative of) NHRIs, each from one of four GANHRI's regional networks, working on a voluntary basis. The current dynamics of the sessions can already be considered too heavy, given the volume of documents associated with each case. Without deep structural and conceptual changes in the accreditation process, it would be impossible to review 16 new accreditations each year, together with all regular reaccreditations. However, one should also consider this indicator was just too ambitious. That does not mean that the accreditation process is perfect. *Au contraire*. It should be enhanced – only for different reasons, which are beyond the scope of this study.

CHAPTER 5

Leaving No One Unaccountable

As argued by GANHRI (2017), given their unique mandate and role, ombuds institutions and other NHRIs can play a key role in the implementation and follow-up of the 2030 Agenda, and are at the core of the SDG 'web of accountability.' In fact, ombuds institutions act as central accountability mechanisms, more generally, including vis-à-vis the security sector, by overseeing and holding to account those in charge of the management, oversight, and provision of security. The six targets covered in this chapter reflect exactly such a role of ombuds institutions, by concentrating on their nature as oversight mechanisms, that is, on making sure that others perform, fulfill, and achieve; and that they are accountable for their actions and failures to act.

Why such a strong emphasis on accountability? Because accountability is essential to effective governance. An effective democratic state relies on legislative, administrative, and judicial institutions, which are empowered to exercise a degree of direct control over how the other institutions exercise their functions. The notion of checks and balances is a constitutional concept, which spans the whole structure and functions of the state. Accountability lies at the very core of the checks and balances system.

The modern state has undergone a reconfiguration of its structure and functions, and new institutions have arisen with control and oversight functions. One of those is the ombuds institution, often regarded as 'a modern mechanism of democratic accountability' (Owen 1993: 1). It serves as an important element of good governance, enhancing the accountability of the government, and in so doing helps to improve the functioning of public administration (Reif 2004: 59).

Due to their specific role, ombuds institutions have the potential to contribute to all three main forms of accountability: horizontal, vertical, and diagonal (Figure 4).

Ombuds institutions can check the abuses by other public agencies and branches of government. This form of oversight or control exercised by one public institution over others is qualified as 'horizontal accountability.' Horizontal accountability requires the existence of

How to cite this book chapter:
Glušac, L. 2023. *Leaving No One Behind, Leaving No One Unaccountable: Ombuds Institutions, Good (Security Sector) Governance and Sustainable Development Goal 16*. Pp. 51–60. London: Ubiquity Press. DOI: https://doi.org/10.5334/bcw.e. License: CC BY-NC 4.0

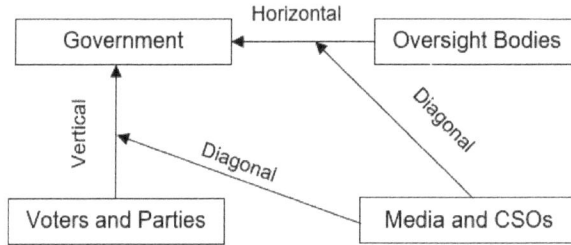

Figure 4: Relationship of accountability subtypes (Lührmann, Marquardt and Mechkova 2020: 812).

institutions – legislative and judicial branches, and other oversight agencies – that can demand information and punish improper behavior (O'Donnell 1998; Rose-Ackerman 1996). In the ombuds case, as noted by Castro, horizontal accountability can take different forms, such as administrative accountability (by reviewing proper conduct including the procedural fairness of bureaucratic acts), legal accountability (by supervising the observance of legal rules), and constitutional accountability (by evaluating whether legislative acts are in accordance with constitutional provisions) (Castro 2019: 8).

Ombuds institutions also act as vertical accountability mechanisms between the public and the government, serving as a channel through which citizens can lodge complaints about the government. Moreover, by assessing the performance of administrative authorities, the ombuds institutions provide feedback on governmental action, helping the government learn from citizens' complaints.

Civil society organizations, independent media, and engaged citizens can use a broad range of actions to provide and amplify information about the government, thereby holding it accountable (Grimes 2013; Lührmann, Marquardt and Mechkova 2020). This form of accountability is usually called diagonal or social. For instance, media reporting can help principals such as voters and legislatures make informed choices and perform additional pressure on public officials, whilst CSOs can directly pressure the government to change a specific policy (Peruzzotti & Smulovitz 2006). As already noted, media and CSOs may also amplify the findings of oversight bodies, including ombuds institutions, and vice versa.

The strong accountability function of the ombuds institutions and their ability to influence both the public decision-making process and the behavior of public authorities have contributed to their acknowledgment as part of the doctrine as a 'fourth power' institution (Addink 2005: 273). As a fourth power, the ombuds institution focuses on institutional integrity. Spigelman (2004: 6–7) writes that institutional integrity goes beyond a narrow concept of legality to concern itself with ensuring that government institutions exercise the powers conferred on them in the manner in which, and for the purposes for which, they are expected or required to do so. He considers fidelity to the public purposes for which the institution was created and the application of the public values that the institution is expected (or required) to obey (Spigelman 2004: 6). In this context, integrity may be understood as compliance with the endorsed legal principles and values intrinsic to the democratic rule of law, including certain principles of good governance (Addink 2015: 30–32). The principle of integrity and discussions around it have inspired some authors, such as Ackerman, to argue that there should be a separate and distinctive constitutional branch of government known as the 'integrity branch' (Ackerman 2000: 691–693). Other authors exploring the new fourth branch include Tushnet (2021), who calls them 'institutions for protecting constitutional democracy,' and Khaitan (2021), who uses the term 'guarantor institutions.'

How does accountability play out in the development context? In short – poorly. Many authors have argued that the traditional separation of human rights and development frameworks has led to the absence of specific human rights accountability in development policy and activities (Bradlow 1996; Darrow 2003; Skogly 2001). Human rights cannot properly be upheld because human rights obligations are not factored into development policies (Mcinerney-Lankford 2009: 74). The absence of legal duties in development policy frameworks, Twomey (2007) argues, undermines the possibility of the key contribution of human rights – accountability – being upheld in the context of development with respect to both process and outcome.

It is true that newer international agreements, such as the Paris Declaration do not *a priori* go against human rights accountability; however, they do not include any corresponding human rights obligations, or human rights impact assessments at least. Mcinerney-Lankford (2009: 75) asserts that 'human rights law norms could deepen and ground existing accountability mechanisms and help fill some of the perceived accountability gaps in both horizontal (state to state) and vertical (state to citizen) relationships.' Such a general trend of the lack of accountability in the development context has, unfortunately, transferred to the 2030 Agenda as well. The neglect of accountability was already clearly reflected in the inter-governmental negotiations leading up to the adoption of the SDGs (Breuer & Leininger 2021: 2). This is, however, not surprising, given the nature of the global regime.

Scholars have, therefore, asserted that accountability can be best pursued through systems for monitoring progress at the national level (Bowen et al. 2017). However, the first cross-national analysis of national horizontal accountability mechanisms to ensure effective SDG implementation has shown that serious formal commitment to accountability in SDGs implementation has been a choice of individual governments rather than a standard in national SDG implementation across countries (Breuer and Leininger 2021: 18). In other words, accountability is only as strong as a country's willingness to submit to accountability.

Despite these first pessimistic results, the national level remains the best *locus*, where real opportunities lie in the accountability mechanisms for the overall implementation of SDGs (Karlsson-Vinkhuyzen, Dahl & Persson 2018: 1385; see also Bowen et al. 2017). Along these lines, Karlsson-Vinkhuyzen and others (2018) have argued that these accountability mechanisms can include: national institutions such as parliaments and audit institutions using their formal mandates to oversee and evaluate government policy; civil society and the media doing the same on more informal mandates; and finally the internal monitoring and evaluation system of the government.

As part of its follow-up and review mechanisms, the 2030 Agenda for Sustainable Development encourages Member States to 'conduct regular and inclusive reviews of progress at the national and sub-national levels, which are country-led and country-driven' (para. 79). These are known as voluntary national reviews (VNRs). They aim to facilitate the sharing of experiences, including successes, challenges, and lessons learned, with a view to accelerating the implementation of the 2030 Agenda. The VNRs also seek to strengthen policies and institutions of governments and to mobilize multi-stakeholder support and partnerships for the implementation of the SDGs. To that end, they can also serve as an accountability tool. Even though these reports are voluntary, almost 180 members of the High-level Political Forum on Sustainable Development (HLPF) have already submitted at least one VNR report. This equates to approximately 90 per cent of UN Member States.

VNRs are most usually prepared by the national SDG coordination body or similar structure. Is there a place for ombuds institutions in VNR structure/process? Some authors (Breuer and Leininger 2021: 10) recommend that ombuds institutions (NHRIs) shall be 'represented either in the national SDG coordination body or in working groups and technical committees collaborating with this body.' This study supports such a view but only if they are members in an advisory capacity. Coopting ombuds institutions in such bodies may affect their independence, so the right distance must be taken, and the government must take full responsibility for the ultimate results. The same applies to a VNR, which should be prepared in a broad consultative process, but the government should also take primary responsibility for its content, and the results therein. Although Breuer and Leininger (2021: 10) claim that NHRIs' 'involvement in the elaboration of their countries' VNRs will add credibility to the national review processes,' this study argues against it. This should be the job of the government. Ombuds institutions may indeed contribute, in particularly by providing data and evidence as input to the national VNR process.

Some authors, such as Maaike de Langen (2021), advocate for a Voluntary Ombuds Review. Such exercise would secure ombuds institutions' independence, but also their active participation in the SDG implementation and reporting processes. Whilst this idea has potential, it remains to be seen whether ombuds institutions would go along this path, considering many already experience reporting fatigue. Besides their obligatory annual reports submitted to the parliament (and sometimes to the government as well), most ombuds institutions have developed the practice of producing special reports, while a considerable percentage also prepare submissions to the UN treaty bodies and regional human rights mechanisms.

To that end, it is perhaps more efficient to redesign and restructure ombuds annual reports to serve a double purpose. The ombuds institution of Costa Rica (Defensoría de los Habitantes de la República – DHR) seems to be on a good track here. As early as 2015–2016, DHR did a detailed analysis of the issues it has historically worked with, concluding that they are directly connected to 14 of the 17 SDGs.

Going beyond VNRs and reporting, the chapter presents the account of what ombuds institutions could and should do to assist the efforts of other branches of power to implement (and oversee the implementation of) six SDG 16 targets. The particular focus is on their oversight and accountability role(s).

Promoting the rule of law and ensuring equal access to justice for all (16.3)

There is an interplay between ombuds institutions and the democratic state governed by the rule of law within which this institution operates. On the one hand, the existence of ombuds institutions as an institution presupposes, to a certain extent at least, the rule of law within a democracy, and on the other hand, their work helps to maintain and fortify the rule of law and democracy (Glušac 2020: 3).

Although it is undeniably among the most important targets in the whole 2030 Agenda, sitting at the very core of all other targets, 16.3 has been criticized for its principle-sounding tone, which prevents its operationalization (Satterthwaite and Dhital 2019). The three indicators set for this target only support this. Satterthwaite and Dhital (2019) have demonstrated that the ambition to 'provide access to justice for all' was radically distorted by the selection of two criminal justice indicators – one on unsentenced detainees and another on crime reporting. This strong focus on the criminal justice system is 'not only out of sync with legal needs studies showing that a majority of people's legal issues are civil rather than criminal, but most importantly, fails to provide an assessment of access to justice from the people's perspective' (Laberge & Touihri 2019: 153). The United Nations later added a third indicator focusing on the proportion of the population who have accessed a formal or informal dispute resolution mechanism in the last two years. This indicator has to be adapted to the national context, as formal and informal mechanisms for dispute resolution vary across jurisdictions. In most countries, these would include formal mechanisms, such as the courts of the police, while in others, they are to be complemented by informal mechanisms, such as customary law mechanisms managed by traditional or religious leaders. Reporting on this indicator should thus include all dispute resolution mechanisms generally recognized and used in the community (UN Stats 2021). This means that ombuds institutions should also be included under this indicator. However, it is yet to be fully operational. Currently, there are no data available for this indicator, including in the most comprehensive databases, such as the SDG Tracker (n.d. B).

Regarding the second part of this target, broadly understood, ombuds institutions can be perceived as justice mechanisms on their own, in the sense they serve to redress unfair decisions and abuses of power. With their comprehensive mandate, accessibility, and visibility to the widest population, they ensure that the rights of marginalized and vulnerable groups are respected. This communicates well with the 'leave no one behind' credo.

From a narrower angle, ombuds institutions' contribution to this target can be analyzed through the lenses of their jurisdiction vis-à-vis the judiciary. To that regard, some ombuds institutions have a stronger role to play than others. Even though most ombuds institutions are not authorized to control the judiciary (neither in terms of intervening in pending court proceedings nor in terms of checking judicial decisions), some legal orders (such as Sweden, Finland, and Poland) provide for an extensive ombuds control of the judiciary, including the substance of judicial decisions, to the same degree as the administrative branch (Castro 2019: 65–66). In other jurisdictions, as in Slovenia, the ombuds institution can intervene in court proceedings in cases, for example, of undue delay and abuse of authority. Still, when ombuds institutions are given some jurisdiction over the judiciary, it is most usually over the administrative conduct of court proceedings (delays, setting down a hearing date, obtaining expert opinions, executed copies, and service of judgments), defaults in executing judgments, deficiencies in court equipment, impolite conduct by officials, and the initiation of disciplinary measures against judges (Castro 2019: 65–66). This is also the standpoint of the Venice Commission (2019: para. 13), which stipulates that 'the competence of the Ombudsman relating to the judiciary shall be confined to ensuring procedural efficiency and administrative functioning of that system.'

A caveat regarding breaches of criminal law is also needed here.[3] Ombuds institutions are not criminal justice authorities; they do not prosecute crimes. However, when in the course of its own investigations, they learn of conduct that may constitute a criminal offence, they are obliged to inform competent authorities. Furthermore, much of the ombuds work is focused on minimizing the chances of criminal offence to occur. For example, by following up on UN treaty body recommendations on family violence or violence against children, ombuds institutions contribute to creating a system that would effectively protect these vulnerable groups and make sure that criminal justice system would act swiftly and efficiently if such a case were to happen. Similarly, by visiting places of detention, ombuds institutions help to prevent torture and to eliminate the culture of impunity for torture.

Reducing illicit financial and arms flows, strengthening the recovery and return of stolen assets, and combating all forms of organized crime (16.4)

Organized crime and illicit arms flow both have a detrimental impact on the security and stability of a state as they threaten the state's monopoly over the legitimate use of coercive force (Castro 2019: 65–66). The contribution of ombuds institutions to achieving this target could primarily be through the oversight of the work of the police, that is, through investigating individual cases. Ombuds institutions may learn of improper behavior of the police or other state authorities included in the fight against organized crime, through media or complaints. Beyond that, ombuds institutions have a limited role to play, except in the case when they have an explicit mandate to curb corruption, which is the focus of the next target (16.5).

Reducing corruption and bribery (16.5)

The ombuds institutions' role in horizontal and vertical accountability coupled with this strong mandate to protect human rights makes them well-placed to play an important function in applying principles of good governance with a view to improving government quality, including the prevention of corruption (McMillan 2004: 7).

---

[3] The author thanks the reviewer for suggesting this addition.

A growing number of countries have entrusted ombuds institutions with an explicit mandate to fight corruption. That has been a trend, particularly in Africa, where Lesotho, Mauritius, Namibia, Rwanda, Seychelles, Ghana, and South Africa (The Public Protector) are among notable cases. When an ombudsman has an anti-corruption mandate, it can provide financial (concerning the misuse of public funds, conflict of interest, etc.) as well as constitutional and administrative accountability (Reif 2004: 60). For instance, in Ghana, the Commission on Human Rights and Administrative Justice (CHRAJ or the Commission) is designated as the coordinating body for the National Anti-Corruption Plan. In this role, the Commission convenes a number of thematic international and national dialogues with relevance to advance issues related to SDG 16, such as promoting the relevance of linking human rights in anti-corruption efforts to, for example, strengthen institutions, ensure rule of law and access to justice, and design adequate policies for asset recovery and return (König-Reis n.d.). Furthermore, the CHRAJ organized a national Conference on Anti-Corruption and Transparency, which gathered high-level officials (including Ghana's Vice-President), and key representatives from the governance and justice sectors, civil society, the UN, and the private sector (König-Reis n.d.). Participants reviewed existing policies and strategies and agreed on measures to strengthen institutions involved in fighting corruption and ensuring transparency and accountability (König-Reis n.d.).

Another interesting trend is designating ombuds institutions as external whistleblowing protection authorities, as in Hungary or Croatia. Most national laws provide for a three-layer protection system – internal, external, and public. Internal whistleblowing is defined as disclosing information to an employer, through a confidential person (authorized person). External whistleblowing is achieved by disclosing information to the external public authority, legally designated for this task. The third type is whistleblowing to the public, which often comes as the last resort.

Although the authorities for external whistleblowing vary across the jurisdiction, in some countries, as in Croatia, the Ombudsman (*Pučki pravobranitelj*) is a designated body. The Ombudsman is authorized to receive a report of irregularities and then forward it to the authorities responsible for dealing with its content while protecting the identity of the whistleblower and the confidentiality of the information contained in the report from unauthorized disclosure or disclosure to other persons unless this is contrary to the law. The authorities authorized to act upon the content of the report (e.g., various inspectorates, the State Attorney's Office, and others) are obliged to report back to the Ombudsman of the action taken on the report within 30 days after receiving it and, within 15 days of ending the procedure, to submit a reasoned report on the final outcome of the procedure. This information is then forwarded by the Ombudsman to the whistleblower.

Whistleblowing is particularly relevant for the security sector. Military whistleblowers face particular challenges: a rigid command structure, rules on discipline, and restrictions on speech with potential criminal consequences for non-compliance (Whistleblowing International Network 2019). The same applies to those whistleblowers coming from the police or intelligence services.

In this context, in its 2010 resolution, the Parliamentary Assembly of the Council of Europe (PACE 2010: para. 6.2) stressed that legislation on whistleblowers should be comprehensive and should cover the private and the public sectors, including members of the armed forces and special services. A 2014 recommendation by the Council of Europe's Committee of Ministers (Council of Europe 2014) noted, however, that in national normative, institutional, and judicial networks established to protect the rights and interests of whistleblowers, special schemes or rules, including modified rights and obligations, may apply to information related to national security or defense.

Such 'special schemes and rules' are widely applied by the Member States, not only of the Council of Europe but of the European Union as well. Before the adoption of the Directive on Whistleblowing in 2019, only 10 EU Member States had comprehensive or fragmented protection systems for whistleblowers (EUROMIL n.d.). The same applies to other jurisdictions where legislation on the protection of whistleblowers simply does not apply to security sector personnel (including military personnel). Often, they are explicitly excluded from the legislation, such as in the United Kingdom or Canada.

Whilst whistleblower protection for security sector employees is virtually non-existent, many countries have adopted robust legislation penalizing the disclosure of state secrets. This varies in form, especially concerning how an 'official secret' is defined. However, national security consistently appears as a reason to bar disclosure and coupled with the lack of whistleblower protection for security sector employees, creates an almost impenetrable fortress of secrecy in security matters (Kagiaros 2015: 410). A similar protection applies to military personnel. They will continue to suffer unnecessarily if countries do not specifically address the importance of protecting military whistleblowers in their national whistleblowing laws (Whistleblowing International Network 2019). Excessive labeling of information as confidential remains the major obstacle for military whistleblowers, severely shrinking their maneuvering space. In cases when they are reporting wrongdoings for the actions/information not classified as secret, military personnel have different options and avenues of action.

In jurisdictions where ombuds institutions are designated as the authorities for external whistleblowing, they should invest efforts in bettering the legal and actual position of the security sector whistleblowers, both in individual cases and more systemically, through advocating for more inclusive legislation, protecting those brave enough to disclose severe irregularities in the security sector institutions.

Developing effective, accountable, and transparent institutions (16.6)

Developing effective, accountable, and transparent institutions may be understood as a supreme goal of ombuds institutions, the ultimate result they strive for. This SDG 16 target covers three principles of good governance that are of the highest importance for good governance – effectiveness, accountability, and transparency. All activities of ombuds institutions aim to contribute to developing such institutions. This is, however, a never-ending task, calling for constant and consistent efforts, on both individual and systemic levels. It is also not by any means an exclusive task of ombuds institutions. It is the responsibility of each public authority to invest efforts in making itself an effective, accountable, and transparent institution. To that end, this target applies to both ombuds institutions themselves, and those institutions they are mandated to oversee.

Although ombuds institutions are widely accepted as important accountability mechanisms, it is less illuminated in the literature that they can also make a substantive contribution to the effectiveness of the security sector. As argued by Born and Geisler Mesevage (2012: 7), good oversight covers elements well beyond the propriety and legality of a security apparatus' activities, including also their effectiveness and efficiency. Unlike some other external state oversight mechanisms, such as the judiciary, which primarily assesses the legality of the work of security institutions (compliance with the law), ombuds institutions can, in addition, actually influence the service's effectiveness and efficiency (Glušac 2018b: 65). This is recognized by ombuds institutions themselves. For instance, in the framework of the annual International Conference of Ombuds Institutions for the Armed Forces (ICOAF), ombuds institutions underlined their important role in contributing to the operational effectiveness of the armed forces they oversee, through upholding individual rights and improving the governance of the defence sector (ICOAF 2021: para. 4). While noting that the scope of the contribution of ombuds institutions to the operational effectiveness of the armed forces varies depending on their particular mandate, ombuds institutions reiterated that they are all well placed to contribute to respecting the legal limits of operational effectiveness (ICOAF 2021: para. 7). To develop effective, accountable, and transparent institutions, collective action with broad stakeholder participation is needed. Collective action is also linked to accountability in the classic 'free rider' problem: actors may be reluctant to participate in collective action towards the implementation of a common goal unless they are confident that progress will be made (Sachs 2012). Developing democratic institutions is notoriously challenging, because years of effort may be diminished in only seconds. It only takes one wrong decision to lose the trust in the process, and lose those 'bandwagoning' free riders, necessary for the ultimate success.

Public institutions are invented to fulfil the needs of the people. However, people around the world suffer from institutions that are ineffective, unjust, exclusive, corrupt, unaccountable, and/ or unresponsive, as well as by-laws, policies, and budgets that are inequitable, discriminatory, or regressive. Not rarely, those are the result of state capture, described as an 'intentionally political undertaking in which individuals and groups (business magnates, politicians, criminals and, as is often the case, all of these together) gradually and systematically rewrite the formal "rules of the game" in order to pursue their particular interests, financial or political, to the detriment of the public good' (Petrović & Pejić Nikić 2020: 7).

In the more advanced stages of state capture, the separation of powers comes to exist in name only, and the institutions of the state cease granting socio-economic, political, and other rights to the citizenry, functioning instead completely in the service of a tight circle of individuals and groups Petrović & Pejić Nikić 2020: 7). Such contexts are characterized by drastically shrunk space for the actions of organized civil society and independent oversight bodies, which operate under constant threat. Insufficient capacity, funding, and/or political autonomy often undermine the role ombuds institutions can play in ensuring governing institutions are accountable, inclusive, rights-based, and capable of investigating and seeking redress for human rights violations (UNDP 2018: 14).

Ensuring responsive, inclusive, participatory, and representative decision-making (16.7)

Ensuring responsive, inclusive, participatory, and representative decision-making essentially means recognizing and achieving diversity. The type(s) of diversity depends on the nature and composition of a given society, meaning that what counts as 'diverse' depends on the existence and recognition of various minorities (gender, ethnic, religious, sexual, etc.).

The United Nations have set two indicators for achieving this target: (1) proportions of positions in national and local institutions, including (a) the legislatures, (b) the public service, and (c) the judiciary, compared to national distributions, by sex, age, persons with disabilities, and population groups; and (2) proportion of the population who believe decision-making is inclusive and responsive, by sex, age, disability, and population group (SDG Tracker n.d. A; Global Indicators n.d.). While not underestimating the importance of other types of diversity, two sub-indicators are of particular importance for this study: gender and minority representations.

National parliaments have traditionally been male-populated. To mitigate this, the world has witnessed the rapid expansion of electoral gender quotas in the past few decades. Such a strategy has informational and normative effects. Public debates on introducing quotas raise individual awareness about the underrepresentation of women (informational effect), while, once adopted, they give a clear signal that persistent gender imbalance is a social problem to be redressed (normative effect). Many studies, including large-scale and regional, have reaffirmed that quotas stimulate support for stronger female representation (Aldrich & Daniel 2020; Clayton & Zetterberg 2018; Dimitrova-Grajzl & Obasanjo 2019). Furthermore, citizens in countries with gender quotas also display stronger support for increased female participation in politics (Fernández & Valiente 2021).

Across Africa, many countries are world leaders in terms of women's representation in parliament with more than a dozen countries having 30 percent women or more in their national legislatures. Such a result is attributed largely to the adoption of an electoral gender quota (Bauer 2021). Research has shown that stronger female representation in African parliaments leads to a number of substantive and symbolic effects. These include the adoption of laws that address women's interests in the areas of gender-based violence, land rights, and family law, and women's enhanced engagement in politics (e.g., voting) (Bauer 2021).

While it should be noted that having more women in parliament has not always led to more democratic polities, it is anticipated that experienced women legislators may contribute to more democratic dispensations in the future (Bauer 2021). Even in authoritarian one-party systems, the researchers found that quotas may result over time in what Joshi and Thimothy (2019) call a delayed integration process featuring a gradual rise of women into arenas of power alongside increasing professionalization and capabilities of women within parliament.

Nonetheless, the potential of the quota system should not be overestimated. In order to empower women and secure their long-term participation and representation, the quota system, as a legislative device usually adopted through elite-driven (top-down) initiatives, should be complemented with a parallel bottom-up process of transforming gendered power relations.

The international human rights regime allows for positive discrimination and positive action measures for people with disabilities and minorities (EQUINET 2014). Assuring minority representation in public administration is a precondition for an inclusive society. In conflict-prone societies, ensuring optimal minority representation in security forces, particularly in the police, should be a strategic goal. Positive action may be a useful strategy to recruit minority talents to work in the police. That especially applies to societies with a history of inter-ethnic violence, even more so if the police have taken part in violent actions. The results of a recent study published in *Science* suggest that diversity reforms can improve police treatment of minority communities (Bocar et al. 2021).

Ombuds institutions can contribute to achieving this target by overseeing the implementation of those positive action measures (including quotas). This particularly applies to advocating for better minority (gender, ethnic, etc.) representation in public administration, where ombuds institutions are expected to have stronger influence, given their jurisdiction and direct access.

They can also take an active part in awareness-raising and advocacy campaigns promoting diversity in the security sector institutions. For instance, there is an opportunity for the Indian National Human Rights Commission to get involved in the discussions (and controversies) around the new recruitment scheme in Indian Armed Forces, called 'Agnipath,' which aims to transform the Indian Armed Forces and decrease the average age of the armed forces personnel, but also with potentially severe consequences on the rights of those new armed forces personnel and their future professional trajectories.

Finally, ombuds institutions should ensure the pluralism of their ranks. Ensuring pluralism is also a requirement for an A-status NHRI, according to the Paris Principles. The Subcommittee on Accreditation notes that there are diverse models for ensuring the requirement of pluralism in the composition of the NHRIs as set out in the Paris Principles (G.O. 1.7. GANHRI SCA 2018). While for the human rights commission, such pluralism may be ensured through the composition of the decision-making body, given that the ombuds institution is most frequently single-headed, pluralism may be demonstrated through the composition of senior management, such as the deputy ombudspersons or secretary-general, who should be representatives of the diverse segments of society (Glušac 2021: 52).

Promoting and enforcing non-discriminatory laws and policies for sustainable development (16.B)

The human rights promise of equality and non-discrimination is at the heart of the 2030 Agenda
—UN High Commissioner for Human Rights (2015)

These were the words of the UN High Commissioner for Human Rights at the UN Summit launching the 2030 Agenda. The words are important as they reiterate the strong nexus between human rights and discrimination. The list of prohibited grounds of discrimination in international human rights law is not only long but is also formulated in open-ended terms to make clear that it applies to evolving forms of discrimination (Winkler & Satterthwaite 2017: 1079).

As with some other SDG 16 targets, there is only one adopted indicator for this global and comprehensive target: the proportion of the population reporting having felt personally discriminated against or harassed in the previous 12 months on the basis of a ground of discrimination prohibited under international human rights law. As argued by Winkler and Satterthwaite (2017: 1079), 'a balance must be struck between over-simplification and demanding disaggregation that overburdens statistical offices.' However, this indicator does not come near striking such a balance. It does not allow monitoring progress for marginalized groups.

In most countries, the protection of equality (anti-discrimination) and of human rights is designated to different state authorities, which testifies to different understandings, discourses, and approaches taken to fulfil these mandates. There are a few exemptions. Examples include the Equality and Human Rights Commission, which promotes and upholds equality and human rights ideals and laws across England, Scotland, and Wales, and the Irish Human Rights and Equality Commission. Both institutions are accredited with A status with GANHRI. Other exemptions include ombuds institutions with explicit human rights mandates, which are also either formally designated as national anti-discrimination (equality) bodies, such as Georgia, Greece, or Montenegro, or not, but still having jurisdiction over different aspects of non-discrimination law within their general human rights mandates, as in Croatia or Lithuania.

Being designated as an explicit equality body or not, ombuds institutions/NHRIs may address systemic problems related to discrimination. They can use their right to provide 'legislative' advice or directly propose law (when having this mandate) that would help eradicate discriminatory legislation. They are also well-placed to report on the status of discriminatory policies and legislation. Ombuds institutions and other NHRIs can take advantage of participating in formulating national SDG indicators. The Human Rights Commission of Mongolia did this during the consultations on national indicators, by recommending drafting and adopting comprehensive anti-discrimination legislation concerning SDG target 16.b and suggesting including each discriminatory ground as a national indicator in line with the international human rights instruments as well as the Declaration of Principles on Equality.

The 2030 Agenda provides a strong narrative for eliminating inequalities and eradicating discrimination. 'Inequalities and discrimination are the defining challenges of our time,' reaffirmed the UN High Commissioner for Human Rights in 2015. A challenge yet to be fully addressed, it seems fair to add.

CHAPTER 6

Conclusion with Recommendations

The 2030 Agenda has given the most ambitious promise – to end poverty, foster peace, safeguard the rights and dignity of all people, and protect the planet. After initial well-deserved euphoria, the reality has struck quickly and hard. Already after a couple of years, the progress of achieving most of the goals was out of the projected rhythm and trajectory.

The current picture is gloomy. Pleas for global peace are growing louder as the world witnesses the highest number of violent conflicts since 1945, with approximately 2 billion people living in conflict-affected countries by the end of 2020, with over 82 million people forcibly displaced worldwide, according to official UN data (UN 2022: para. 148). Those numbers do not even include internally displaced people and refugees from Ukraine. The costs of war and conflict are high, affecting the poorest and most vulnerable the most, and leading to global impact and escalating humanitarian needs (UN 2022: para. 148).

Those poor, disadvantaged, and marginalized communities remain left behind, with the least say in the decisions that affect them, and are least likely to be included in the data and evidence governments use to allocate resources and shape policies. At the same time, the space for civic action, fundamental freedoms, and meaningful participation is shrinking drastically in countries around the world (Freedom House 2022).

In times of conflict, societies rarely (if ever) become more democratic. However, many inherently democratic institutions have, historically, originated from the conflict, or because of the conflict. Ombuds institutions are one of these. The world's first-ever (proto)ombuds institution emerged in response to armed conflict. In 1709, after his defeat by Russian Emperor Peter the Great in the Battle of Poltava, Swedish King Charles XII took refuge near Bender, in present-day Moldova, at the invitation of Ottoman rulers who also viewed the Russian Emperor as an enemy. During the almost decade-long exile of Charles, Sweden was in crisis, suffering from poverty, plagues, depleted resources, the dangers of the ongoing war, and widespread corruption. Charles was aware that Sweden was in dire straits and, guided by a coterie of advisors, initiated a

How to cite this book chapter:
Glušac, L. 2023. *Leaving No One Behind, Leaving No One Unaccountable: Ombuds Institutions, Good (Security Sector) Governance and Sustainable Development Goal 16.* Pp. 61–68. London: Ubiquity Press. DOI: https://doi.org/10.5334/bcw.f. License: CC BY-NC 4.0

series of policy and administrative reforms that, among other things, resulted in the creation of a new institution – the King's Ombudsman. A hundred years later, in 1809, Sweden adopted the new constitution, inaugurating the world's first Parliamentary Ombudsman. Though that first (proto)ombuds institution may never have emerged were it not for war, neither its 1809 successor nor its contemporary offshoots were or are meant to be war actors. Ombuds institutions are built for peace. However, they have learned to survive in hostile environments.

Today, ombuds institutions continue operating in diverse environments, from (a decreasing number of) mature democracies to hybrid regimes to fully fledged autocratic regimes. In the latter context, the ombuds institution should be 'an institutional opposition to the authoritarian government, given that the reasons for its establishment go directly against the nature of the authoritarian government' (Glušac 2019b: 503). Ombuds institutions have to fight strongly and persistently to avoid the destiny of other critical voices of dissent against authoritarian manifestations with less formal and social power, such as human rights defenders. The latter are being silenced, detained, and ostracized, worldwide.

Many people remain oppressed and/or invisible to their governments, which reinforces and perpetuates the disadvantages certain groups and people face. As argued by UNDP, this 'erodes the social contract between the state and the people and makes it harder for governments to identify challenges, enact solutions and build the trust, legitimacy and mutual understanding that are among the basic building blocks of effective, equitable and inclusive governance' (UNDP 2018: 14).

The 2030 Agenda has formulated global goals meant to be implemented primarily by national authorities to the ultimate benefit of the people on the local level. Being well-trained to apply international standards to the national (local) context, ombuds institutions could serve as a social fiber of SSR and SDG efforts. In the right environment, they could help build trust between international and national actors, liaising between them when frictions occur, and making sure that all social forces are included in the process, and their needs and interests are duly considered.

This study demonstrated that not many ombuds institutions worldwide have formally integrated the 2030 Agenda into their work. Yet, this does not mean they do not understand their role in contributing to achieving SDGs, they just do not brand their activities, findings, and results as such. This book showed that existing (academic and policy) literature has mostly described the role of ombuds institutions/NHRIs in achieving the SDGs in terms of enablers, bridges, and data providers. Although correct, these characterizations fail to capture their full potential in the realization of SDG 16. Hence, the main goal of this study was to try to go beyond such generic descriptions and dive more deeply to see how these institutions could contribute to each of the 12 SDG 16 targets. The central assumption was that ombuds institutions can indeed contribute to achieving all SDG 16 targets, although their impact naturally varies from one target to another.

In line with that, this study divided the potential contribution of ombuds institutions to the realization of SDG 16 into two analytical categories entitled 'leaving no one behind' and 'leaving no one unaccountable.' The former focused on all those who endure disadvantages or deprivations that limit their choices and opportunities relative to others in society. It thus concentrated on the targets to which ombuds institutions actively and directly contribute. These primarily relate to human rights, anti-discrimination, access to justice, reducing violence, and similar. The latter referred to those targets to whose realization ombuds institutions can contribute indirectly, by working with, pressuring, and making public administration accountable, in cases when the administration as the primary duty-bearer fails to protect the rights of citizens and when their actions fall short of the standards needed to achieve the SDGs. What follows is the summary of the main findings in the form of recommendations.

Given the focus of this research, all recommendations relate to ombuds institutions, either directly or indirectly. The summary starts with broader recommendations aimed at the legislature and the executive which should provide for a proper legal and factual environment for both the security sector and ombuds institutions. The next set of recommendations targets stakeholders, such as CSOs, media, and international organizations. The conclusion then moves on to present recommendations aiming at the nexus between ombuds institutions and security providers, and what the latter should do to contribute more actively to realizing SDG 16, before closing with specific recommendations to ombuds institutions. All recommendations are associated with specific SDG 16 targets, to the greatest degree possible.

Recommendations to the legislature and executive

Listen and amplify; it's your inner voice talking (16.6 and 16.7)

Parliaments are sometimes regarded as the institutional parent of ombuds institutions (Glušac 2019a: 534). This is a useful parallel, given that the parliaments are responsible for providing ombuds institutions with essential preconditions for their establishment and institutional development, including a strong mandate, sufficient capacity, funding, and independence, so they can be capable of investigating and seeking redress for human rights violations, and ensuring government institutions are accountable. Besides being there to enable ombuds institutions' unhindered operations, parliaments should actively benefit from their work by seeking expert advice.

As demonstrated in this study, ombuds institutions are, by rule, appointed and supervised by the parliament to which they report. In fact, in a number of countries, the designation 'parliamentary' is even explicitly included in the official title of the ombuds institution to make this strong institutional connection as clear as possible. This is the reason why ombuds institutions are also called parliament's 'extended arm.'

Parliaments should thus not just listen to but also amplify and put into action the findings of ombuds institutions. They should use the occasions of debating their annual and special reports to put special emphasis on the SDG-connected issues, push governments to implement ombuds' recommendations, and make the best use of their findings.

Frictions between governments and ombuds institutions occur regularly. In such circumstances, parliaments should protect ombuds institutions since the legislative branch of government is institutionally positioned as their key supporter and partner. Yet, given the usual dominance of the executive over the legislature, it is not rare that the parliaments join campaigns against ombuds institutions (as in Poland most recently), labeling them as outlaws and adversaries (Glušac 2020: 2). When they do so, they sever their own arm.

Don't shoot the messenger; change the reality (16.6 and 16.7)

Uniquely positioned in between three branches of government, with their fact-based and objective scrutiny of public administration, ombuds institutions constantly remind the executive of its legal obligations. Ombuds institutions and governments should be natural partners, not competitors or adversaries. Ombuds institutions exist to oversee, not to serve as applauding committees. Oversight usually comes with critical tones. In democracies, the government sees institutional critics of the ombuds institution as an instrument to enhance its work, while autocracy-prone governments often neglect or label such critics as political opposition, avoiding responding to it with arguments (Glušac 2018c: 322).

Ombuds institutions are often bearers of bad news. However, they only *bring* bad news and rarely *create* bad news. They reveal human rights violations and improper administrative behavior, and identify inefficient laws and administrative procedures, etc. Governments should concentrate on eliminating the reasons behind bad news rather than shooting the messenger. After all, the problem will almost certainly not go away by ignoring it, and the bad news will continue to reappear.

Recommendations to stakeholders

To OHCHR and GANHRI: protect the integrity of the accreditation process (16.8 and 16.A)

The SDG Agenda has set a goal that all UN Member States have an A-status NHRI by 2030. This study explained why this is impossible to achieve. It may be even dangerous to try to achieve it. A potential flood of applications for accreditations coupled with the pressure of reaching the SDG indicator could have a detrimental effect on the legitimacy and integrity of the accreditation process conducted by GANHRI's SCA.

However, so far, the trend of new applications has looked more like a drought than a flood, with a very limited number of new applications. The Office of the UN High Commissioner of Human Rights, as the guarantor of the accreditation process, and GANHRI, as an implementor, should monitor the developments closely to assure that the highest and equal standards are applied in each and every case. The peer-review nature of NHRI accreditation is a rather unique feature in the global structures. It should be preserved. So too its integrity.

To civil society organizations: confront ill-performing ombuds institutions (16.6 and 16.10)

Most ombuds institutions are human rights champions. Many of them operate in extreme environments. Yet, they have proven to be resilient and perform well. Some have, however, sided with the oppressive regimes or just gone silent. Strong ombudspersons have to invest immense efforts to create strong institutions. Weak ombudspersons can, however, destroy strong ombuds institutions much more easily. In those cases, civil society should raise concerns about the performance of the ombuds institution. They should insist on debating ombuds institutions' reports in parliament, comparing them to findings from other human rights actors. CSOs may use those opportunities to challenge ombuds institutions' findings. They can do the same by preparing their own reports, aimed either at the domestic public or at international human rights bodies, such as the UN treaty bodies or regional human rights mechanisms (Glušac 2020: 2). Submitting shadow reports to the GANHRI's SCA may be a very effective way of pressing ombuds institutions to perform better. CSOs may submit shadow reports on the performance of ombuds institutions under review, which have an opportunity to respond to such reports during the accreditation process, and questions to ombuds institutions can also be based on information received from CSOs (Glušac 2020: 2).

To the media: act as a megaphone (16.1, 16.3, and 16.10)

Media associations should work with ombuds institutions to organize trainings for journalists on how to report on human rights issues, particularly on gender and family violence and when children are involved.

Ombuds institutions should use the media as their megaphones and as a pressuring channel. Often the public officials react to ombuds' requests and recommendations only after being pressured by media reports. Cooperation with media outlets (traditional and electronic) is essential for ombuds institutions' ability to conduct large-scale advocacy, awareness-raising, and educational campaigns.

In return, ombuds institutions should pay particular attention to protecting the rights of the media workers (journalists, editors, etc.), as they are often subject to threats and attacks coming from various sources, including government officials and the criminal milieu. This includes monitoring all places of detention to make sure that no arbitrary detention and torture occur.

Recommendations to security providers and ombuds institutions

Build trust and professional ethos; embrace the oversight (16.3 and 16.6)

Though it may seem that an intrinsic interest of security actors is to avoid oversight and account-ability, ombuds institutions and other oversight actors should invest their efforts in explaining that they are actually good partners of a good security institution (Glušac 2018b: 66). The security apparatus should embrace the oversight, because when the ombuds institution determines, for instance, that a security service has applied special investigative measures fully in accordance with the law, such a confirmation can only raise their credibility and trust among citizens. National security is thus a reason for inclusion, not exclusion, of ombuds institutions (Glušac 2018b: 62). The ultimate goal of oversight of the security sector, particularly in countries with an authoritarian history, is to build a professional *ethos* of security sector personnel that would value oversight as a means of advancing their work (Glušac 2018b: 66). This is a two-way street. With their objective and professional conduct, ombuds institutions can instill confidence, proving to security services that they are valuable and necessary partners and not *a priori* a nemesis (Glušac 2018b: 66).

Abandon the false freedom-security dilemma (16.3 and 16.6)

The security sector and ombuds institutions should work together on promoting a view that a rela-tionship between security and liberty (human rights) is symbiotic rather than conflicting (Glušac 2018b: 66). Democratic institutions serve to bring both freedom and security to their constituen-cies. Democratic institutions should thus be understood and pursued as a value, not a policy goal.

Embrace diversity (16.7 and 16.B)

This research demonstrated the importance of positive action measures, such as parliamentary gender quotas and special employment programs for minorities, for the overall fight against discrimination and inequalities.

Security providers should embrace such diversity because it helps them to better understand the society they serve to protect. Security institutions should ideally mirror the structure of society.

Ombuds institutions should oversee the implementation of those positive action measures. They can also work together with security sector institutions in making sure that inclusive-ness and diversity are properly understood and implemented in the specific environment of the security sector.

Watch for the early signals of conflict (16.1)

Being present at the local level and engaging with local communities and stakeholders is also a prerequisite to recognizing early signs of conflict, particularly in multiethnic and multireligious societies.

Local police and military chiefs should be chosen among those officers most respected in local communities. Mediation and offering good services are two rewarding avenues for working with local community leaders and national actors to resolve conflicts in the early stages of conflict or post-conflict settings, especially when security forces (military and/or armed police) are deployed on the ground. Being independent and impartial, ombuds institutions should work on building stronger ties and confidence with local communities, to be able to bring different social forces to the table and foster dialogue.

Help remove the cloak of invisibility (16.9)

Whilst they are out there, many people do not formally exist. They are not registered, nor do they have personal documents. As demonstrated in the case of Serbia, ombuds institutions are well-placed to actively contribute to protecting the right to legal identity, particularly in contexts where the procedure of providing proof of legal identity is not legally or procedurally fully regulated. They can, hence, help create legal and procedural preconditions for eradicating the problem of legally invisible people.

Security providers also play a critical role in this endeavor. In many cases those newly registered citizens have to go through a vetting procedure. The police and security service should make sure that those procedures are well-regulated, efficient, and transparent (to the greatest degree possible), guaranteeing procedural fairness. These identification and registration systems should be introduced with the purpose of inclusion, not exclusion, of stateless people or those with no personal documents.

Recommendations to ombuds institutions specifically

Do not take on the role of the executive, but do provide data (16.3 and 16.7)

Being independent, ombuds institutions may choose on their own how they implement SDGs in their own work and if and how they are to be involved in the government actions. In situations when governments do little or nothing to implement the SDGs, ombuds institutions may be tempted to step in and lead the process. This study advocated for a different approach, meaning that that ombuds institutions' main role should be to support and contribute, not to lead. Ombuds institutions should be there to advise their governments, correct their actions, and advance both legislation and practice. They should be hesitant to take on the tasks of the executive. It is the job of the executive to take the lead in implementing the SDGs at the national level, including by creating the national implementation and reporting structures.

Ombuds institutions could, however, join forces with the national SDG coordination body and/or competent authorities, such as national statistical offices, to discuss and design new datasets needed for the SDG implementation and the VNR reporting. They should use this opportunity to advocate for the inclusion of more human rights-based indicators in the national SDG strategies. Annual and other reports of ombuds institutions could serve as indicators or the means of verification at the national level.

Ombuds institutions should use this process to reevaluate and strengthen their own capacity to collect, analyze, and present data. This may reveal the need to acquire new equipment and/or develop new tools, which may be expensive. It is expected that the donor community would be interested to support such projects, given their intended contribution to the national SDG efforts, wider positive implications, and sustainability.

Go viral, go local (16.6 and 16.10)

The COVID-19 pandemic only reiterated the importance of internet access, as many public services were forced to cancel in-person access to their offices. Ombuds institutions should double their efforts to become more accessible through online services, including by being more present on social media channels and testing instant messaging applications as ways of communicating with citizens. Such channels could be used even for lodging complaints as long as they are not submitted merely in the form of a text (chat), but by uploading a filled-in complaint form, available on the ombuds institutions' website. Insisting (whenever possible) on filling in a complaint form is beneficial for both complainant and the ombuds institutions. This encourages potential complainants to think more thoroughly about the problem they have faced and what action they have already taken, and instructs them to provide supporting documents, which all immensely help the ombuds institution to decide on the case more expeditiously. Still, ombuds institutions should not make filling in detailed forms obligatory, to avoid discouraging persons with difficulties in expressing themselves.

Making themselves more visible and accessible online should not be at the expense of ombuds institutions' presence on the ground. Ombuds institutions must be present on the local level to be able to identify the most common problems the citizens face and to be at their disposal as a remedial and complaint mechanism. Decentralizing their work should be a high priority of ombuds institutions, to avoid the perception of an ivory tower institution stuck in the country's capital.

Give children and youth a voice (16.2)

Ombuds institutions should explore ways of including children and youth directly in their work. Creating a Young Advisors Panel or similar structure has proven to be a promising initiative for championing the principle of participation. The main role of such panels is to convey to ombuds institutions the topics that are important to children and young people, point out the problems they face, present their views, and raise issues that are important in improving the position of children and youth in a given country.

Furthermore, ombuds institutions should invest efforts in conducting in-depth inquiries on the topics of particular importance for the well-being of children, such as child trafficking and child beggary, both highly relevant for the realization of the SDGs.

Protect the whistleblowers (16.5)

Ombuds institutions could explore the possibility to advocate for being designated as external whistleblowing protection authorities, as in Croatia.

In jurisdictions where ombuds institutions are designated as the authorities for external whistleblowing, they should invest particular efforts in bettering the legal and actual position of the security sector whistleblowers, both in individual cases and more systemically, through advocating for more inclusive legislation, protecting those brave enough to disclose severe irregularities in the security sector institutions.

***

It is hoped that this research will prove to be valuable to ombuds institutions and their partners, in their efforts to fulfil their mandate and contribute to the 2030 Agenda, as a global set of goals. This study was not only about ombuds institutions, but also about their environment, both legal and institutional. Throughout this research, the nexus between ombuds institutions and other actors was explored, including parliaments, governments, other independent oversight bodies, civil society organizations, and international actors, such as the United Nations or GANHRI. This needs to be stressed, because ombuds institutions can be neither a panacea for all human rights-related problems, nor a replacement for other mechanisms of protection, control, and oversight. Their raison d'être can only be fulfilled in synergy with other functional stakeholders. In other words, ombuds institutions can help rectify systemic and individual deficiencies in the work of public authorities, by increasing the effectiveness of their work and strengthening human rights guarantees, but only in a state where democratic order and a system of checks and balances has been established (Glušac 2017: 67). To achieve this, establishing close partnerships is necessary.

The same applies to achieving the 2030 Agenda. It requires partnership; it requires joining forces. There is no other way to realize this set of ambitious, far-reaching, and comprehensive goals. It was actually the lack of partnership and of common effort that brought the world to this point. The mere existence of the 2030 Agenda is evidence of failure. If the world community had managed to fulfil the Millennium Development Goals, there would not have been the need to come up with the SDGs. Yet, the SDGs are also proof of a devotion to persist and to change, and a commitment to make this planet a better place.

Is the world on good track to achieve the 2030 Agenda? No. States have already underperformed in the first five years of implementation. With the COVID-19 pandemic, slow progress was only replaced with a steady regress. And then the Russian aggression on Ukraine happened. It is very unlikely that the SDGs will be achieved by 2030. However, they are indeed a set of universal goals the world should strive for. Beyond 2030. The SDGs provide a destination, and it is up to the states and other actors to find the best route to it.

Reference List

Ackerman, B. (2000). The new separation of powers. *Harvard Law Review, 113*(3), 691–693. DOI: https://doi.org/10.2307/1342286

Addink, G. H. (2005). The Ombudsman as the fourth power: On the foundations of Ombudsman law from a comparative perspective. In E.C.H.J. van der Linden & F.A.M. Stroink (Eds.), *Judicial lawmaking and administrative law*. Antwerp: Intersentia.

Addink, G. H. (2014). Three legal dimensions of good governance. Some recent developments. In A. Castro (Ed.), *Buen gobierno y derechos humanos*. Lima: Facultad de Derecho PUCP – Idehpucp.

Addink, G. H. (2015). *Good governance in EU member states* (report). Utrecht: Utrecht University. Retrieved from https://dspace.library.uu.nl/bitstream/handle/1874/327316/final_version _september_2015.pdf?sequence=1&isAllowed=y

Addink, G. H. (2019a). Good governance. Concept and context. Oxford: Oxford University Press.

Addink, G. H. (2019b). Good governance: A norm for the administration or a citizen's right?. *Advances in Social Science, Education and Humanities Research, 363*, 1–11. https://www.atlantis -press.com/article/125922691.pdf

Ajana, B. (2013). Governing through biometrics: The biopolitics of identity. London: Palgrave Macmillan.

Aldrich, A. S., & Daniel, W. T. (2020). The consequences of quotas: Assessing the effect of varied gender quotas on legislator experience in the European Parliament. *Politics & Gender, 16*(3), 738–767. DOI: https://doi.org/10.1017/S1743923X19000291

Alexy, R. (2010). A theory of constitutional rights. New York: Oxford University Press.

Alliance of Organization for Human Rights (AOHR). (2021). *Rights defenders under threat in Ecuador: How government protection is insufficient and favors industry interests*. Retrieved from https://www.amazonfrontlines.org/m3di4/Rights-Defenders-Under-Threat-in-Ecuador _-How-Government-Protection-is-Insufficient-and-Favors-Industry-Interests-web.pdf

Apaza, C. (2009). Measuring governance and corruption through the worldwide governance indicators: Critiques, responses, and ongoing scholarly discussion. *Political Science & Politics, 42*(1), 139–43. DOI: https://doi.org/10.1017/S1049096509090106

Arndt, C., & Oman, C. (2006). Uses and abuses of governance indicators. Paris: OECD Development Centre.

Avila, H. (2007). Theory of legal principles. Dordrecht: Springer.

Baldwin, D. A. (1997). The concept of security. *Review of International Studies 23*(1), 5–26.

Ball, N. (1998). Spreading good practices in security sector reform: Policy options for the British government. London: Safer World.

Bartram, J., Brocklehurst, C., Bradley, D., Muller. M., & Evans, B. (2018). Policy review of the means of implementation targets and indicators for the sustainable development goal for water and sanitation. *NPJ Clean Water, 1*(3), 1–5. DOI: https://doi.org/10.1038/s41545-018-0003-0

Bauer, G. (2021). Women in African parliaments: Progress and prospects. In O. Yacob-Haliso & T. Falola (Eds.), *The Palgrave handbook of African women's studies*. Cham: Palgrave Macmillan. DOI: https://doi.org/10.1007/978-3-030-28099-4_122

Beduschi, A. (2019). Digital identity: Contemporary challenges for data protection, privacy and non-discrimination rights. *Big Data & Society 6*(2), 1–6. DOI: https://doi.org/10.1177/2053951719855091

Belgrade Principles (2012, February 22–23). *Belgrade principles on the relationship between national human rights institutions and parliaments* (adopted at the International Seminar on the Relationship between National Human Rights Institutions (NHRIs) and Parliaments. Belgrade, Serbia.

Besançon, M. (2003). *Good governance rankings: The art of measurement* (WPF Reports, No. 36). Cambridge: World Peace Foundation and WPF Program on Intrastate Conflict and Conflict Resolution, Harvard University.

Bocar, B., Knox, D., Mummolo, J., & Rivera, R. (2021). The role of officer race and gender in police-civilian interactions in Chicago. *Science, 371*(6530), 696–702. DOI: https://doi.org/10.1126/science.abd8694

Born, H., & Geisler Mesevage, G. (2012). Introducing intelligence oversight. In H. Born & A. Wills (Eds.), *Overseeing intelligence services: A toolkit* (pp. 3–24). Geneva: DCAF.

Born, H., Wills, A., & Buckland, B. S. (2011). *A comparative perspective of ombudsman institutions for the armed forces* (Policy Paper No. 34). Geneva: DCAF. Retrieved from https://www.dcaf.ch/comparative-perspective-ombudsman-institutions-armed-forces

Born, H., & Wills, A. (Eds.). (2012). Overseeing intelligence services: A toolkit. Geneva: DCAF.

Botchway, F. (2001). Good governance: The old, the new, the principle and the elements. *Florida Journal of International Law, 13*(2), 159–210.

Bowen, K.J., Cradock-Henry, N.A., Koch, F., Patterson, J., Häyhä, T., Vogt, J., Barbi, F. (2017). Implementing the 'Sustainable Development Goals': Towards addressing three key governance challenges—collective action, trade-offs, and accountability. *Current Opinion in Environmental Sustainability, 26*(17), 90–96. DOI: https://doi.org/10.1016/j.cosust.2017.05.002

Bradlow, D. (1996). The World Bank, the IMF and human rights. *Transnational Law and Contemporary Problems, 6*(1), 47–90. https://digitalcommons.wcl.american.edu/cgi/viewcontent.cgi?article=1942&context=facsch_lawrev

Breuer, A., & Leininger, J. (2021). Horizontal accountability for SDG implementation: A comparative cross-national analysis of emerging national accountability regimes. *Sustainability, 13*(3), 7002. DOI: https://doi.org/10.3390/su13137002

Buckland, B. S., & McDermott, W. (2012). Ombuds institutions for the Armed Forces: A handbook. Geneva: DCAF.

Caballero, P. (2019). The SDGs: Changing how development is understood. *Global Policy 10* (Supplement 1), 138–140.

Cardenas, S. (2014). Chains of justice: The global rise of state institutions for human rights. Philadelphia: University of Pennsylvania Press.

Carver, R. (2012). National human rights institutions in central and eastern Europe. In R. Goodman & T. Pegram (Eds.), *Human rights, state compliance, and social change: Assessing national human rights institutions* (pp. 181–209). Cambridge: Cambridge University Press.

Castro, A. (2019). Principles of good governance and the ombudsman. Cambridge: Intersentia.

Center for Economic and Social Rights (CESR). (2016). *From disparity to dignity: Tackling economic inequality through the Sustainable Development Goals* (CESR Human Rights Policy Brief). Retrieved from https://cesr.org/sites/default/files/disparity_to_dignity_SDG10.pdf

Chandler, D. (2007). The security–development nexus and the rise of "anti-foreign policy." *Journal of International Relations and Development, 10*(4), 362–386. DOI: https://doi.org/10.1057/palgrave.jird.1800135

Chesterman, S. (2007). Ownership in theory and practice: Transfer of authority in UN statebuilding operations. *Journal of Intervention and Statebuilding, 1*(1), 3–26. DOI: https://doi.org/10.1080/17502970601075873

Clayton, A., & Zetterberg, P. (2018). Quota shocks: Electoral gender quotas and government spending priorities worldwide. *The Journal of Politics, 80*(3), 916–932.

Council of Europe Commissioner for Human Rights. (2015). *Democratic and Effective Oversight of National Security Services* (Issue paper prepared by Aidan Wills). Strasbourg: Council of Europe.

Council of Europe. (2008). *12 principles of good democratic governance.* Retrieved from https://rm.coe.int/12-principles-brochure-final/1680741931

Council of Europe. (2014, April 30). *Recommendation CM/Rec(2014)7 of the Committee of Ministers on the Protection of Whistleblowers.*

Dahlvik, J., & Pohn-Weidinger, A. (2021). Access to administrative justice and the role of outreach measures: Empirical findings on the Austrian Ombudsman Board. *International Journal of Law in Context, 17*(4), 473–493. DOI: https://doi.org/10.1017/S1744552321000501

Dahlvik, J. (2022). Access to administrative justice in the digital era: Contact possibilities and the personal encounter in public ombuds institutions worldwide. *Recht der Werkelijkheid. Journal of Empirical Research on Law in Action, 43*(2), 48–67. DOI: https://doi.org/10.5553/RdW/138064242022043002004

Danish Institute for Human Rights (DIHR). (2019). National human rights institutions as a driving force for sustainable development: Good practices for SDG programming and monitoring. Copenhagen: DIHR.

Danish Institute for Human Rights (DIHR). (2020). Working with the 2030 Agenda to promote human rights: NHRI initiatives in the Asia Pacific region. Copenhagen: DIHR.

Danish Institute for Human Rights (DIHR) & GANHRI. (2019). *National human rights institutions: Accelerators, guarantors and indicators of sustainable development.* Retrieved from https://www.humanrights.dk/sites/humanrights.dk/files/media/migrated/a4_guarantors_.pdf

Darrow, M. (2003). Between light and shadow: The World Bank, the IMF and international human rights law. Oxford: Hart.

DCAF – Geneva Centre for Security Sector Governance. (2015). *Security sector governance* (SSR Backgrounder Series). Geneva: DCAF.

DCAF – Geneva Centre for Security Sector Governance. (2017). *Ombuds institutions for the armed forces: Selected case studies.* Geneva: DCAF.

DCAF (Geneva Centre for Security Sector Governance) (2019) *Ombuds institutions for the armed forces.* SSR Backgrounder Series, Geneva: DCAF. https://www.dcaf.ch/sites/default/files/publications/documents/DCAF_BG_14_OmbudsInstitutions_Nov2022.pdf

DCAF – Geneva Centre for Security Sector Governance. (2021). *Sustainable Development Goal 16: The importance of good security sector governance for the achievement of the 2030 Agenda* (SSR Backgrounder Series). Geneva: DCAF.

De Beco, G., & Murray, R. (2015). A commentary on the UN Paris principles on national human rights institutions. Cambridge: Cambridge University Press.

De Langen, Maaike. (2021). *Eight ways ombuds institutes can contribute to the SDGs.* SDG Knowledge Hub. Retrieved from http://sdg.iisd.org/commentary/guest-articles/eight-ways-ombuds-institutes-can-contribute-to-the-sdgs/

Dimitrova-Grajzl, V., & Obasanjo, I. (2019). Do parliamentary gender quotas decrease gender inequality? The case of African countries. *Constitutional Political Economy, 30,* 149–176. DOI: https://doi.org/10.1007/s10602-018-09272-0

Donais, T. (2009). Inclusion or exclusion? Local ownership and security sector reform. *Studies in Social Justice, 3*(1), 117–131. DOI: https://doi.org/10.26522/ssj.v3i1.1027

Dörffel, C., & Schuhmann, S. (2022). What is inclusive development? Introducing the multidimensional inclusiveness index. *Social Indicators Research. 162,* 1117–1148. DOI: https://doi.org/10.1007/s11205-021-02860-y

Dursun-Özkanca, O., & Vandemoortele, A. (2012). The European Union and security sector reform: Current practices and challenges of implementation. *European Security, 21*(2), 139–160. DOI: https://doi.org/10.1080/09662839.2012.665881

Dursun-Özkanca, O. (2018). The European Union rule of law mission in Kosovo: An analysis from the local perspective. *Ethnopolitics, 17*(1), 71–94. DOI: https://doi.org/10.1080/17449057.2017.1339456

Dursun-Özkanca, O. (2021). The nexus between security sector governance/reform and Sustainable Development Goal-16: An examination of conceptual linkages and policy recommendations. London: Ubiquity Press. DOI: https://doi.org/10.5334/bcm.b

Edmunds, T. (2002). Security sector reform: Concepts and implementation. In W. N. Germann & T. Edmunds (Eds.), *Towards security sector reform in post Cold War Europe: A framework for assessment* (pp. 15–30). Baden-Baden: Nomos.

Ejdus, F. (2012). Concept of security sector reform. In M. Hadžić, B. Milosavljević, S. Stojanović and F. Ejdus (Eds.), *Yearbook of security sector reform in Serbia* (pp. 61–68). Belgrade: Belgrade Centre for Security Policy.

Ejdus, F. (2017). Here is your mission, now own it! The rhetoric and practice of local ownership in EU interventions. *European Security, 26*(4), 461–484. DOI: https://doi.org/10.1080/09662839.2017.1333495

ENNHRI. (2015). *The Kyiv declaration on the role of national human rights institutions in conflict and post-conflict situations.* Retrieved from http://ennhri.org/wp-content/uploads/2019/10/the_kyiv_declaration.pdf

EQUINET. (2014). *Positive action measures: The experience of equality bodies.* Brussels: EQUINET. Retrieved from https://equineteurope.org/wp-ontent/uploads/2019/07/positive_action_measures_final_with_cover.pdf

EUROMIL. (n.d.). *Human rights jurisprudence in relation to the armed forces.* Retrieved from http://euromil.org/human-rights-jurisprudence-in-relation-to-the-armed-forces/

European Ombudsman. (1997). Annual Report 1997. *Brussels: European Ombudsman.* Retrieved from www.ombudsman.europa.eu/report97/pdf/en/rap97_en.pdf

Fernández, Juan J., & Valiente, C. (2021). Gender quotas and public demand for increasing women's representation in politics: An analysis of 28 European countries. *European Political Science Review, 13*(3), 351–370. DOI: https://doi.org/10.1017/S1755773921000126

Ferris, C., Goodman, B., & Mayer, G. (1980). *Brief on the Office of the Ombudsman* (Occasional Paper No. 6). International Ombudsman Institute. Retrieved from https://www.theioi.org/downloads/epr4c/IOI%20Canada_Occasional%20Paper%2006_Charles%20Ferris_Brief%20on%20the%20Office%20of%20the%20OM_EN_1980.pdf

Freedom House. (2022). Freedom in the world 2022. Retrieved from https://freedomhouse.org/sites/default/files/2022-02/FIW_2022_PDF_Booklet_Digital_Final_Web.pdf

Fukuda-Parr, S. (2014). Global goals as a policy tool: Intended and unintended consequences. *Journal of Human Development and Capabilities, 15*(2–3), 118–131. DOI: https://doi.org/10.1080/19452829.2014.910180

Fukuda-Parr, S. (2015, December 22). It's about values: Human rights norms and tolerance for inequality. 22 December. Open Democracy. Retrieved from https://www.opendemocracy.net/en/openglobalrights-openpage/it-s-about-values-human-rights-norms-and-tolerance-for-inequalit/

Gallie, W. B. (1956). Essentially contested concepts. *Proceedings of the Aristotelian Society, 56,* 167–198.

GANHRI (n.d.). *NHRI accreditation list.* Retrieved from https://www.ohchr.org/sites/default/files/Documents/Countries/NHRI/StatusAccreditationChartNHRIs.pdf

GANHRI. (2017). *National human rights institutions engaging with the Sustainable Development Goals (SDGs).* Geneva: GANHRI. Retrieved from https://ganhri.org/wp-content/uploads/2019/12/GANHRI_NHRIs-engaging-with-the-SDGs_UpdatedVersion.pdf

GANHRI SCA. (2018). *General observations of the sub-committee on accreditation.* Retrieved from https://www.ohchr.org/sites/default/files/Documents/Countries/NHRI/GANHRI/EN_GeneralObservations_Revisions_adopted_21.02.2018_vf.pdf

GANHRI. (2022, June 17). *Upcoming accreditation sessions.* Retrieved from https://ganhri.org/upcoming-sessions/

GANHRI. (2023). *Bureau members.* Retrieved from https://ganhri.org/bureau-members/

Gisselquist, R. M. (2012). *Good governance as a concept, and why this matters for development policy* (WIDER Working Paper, No. 2012/30). The United Nations University World Institute for Development Economics Research (UNU-WIDER), Helsinki. Retrieved from https://www.wider.unu.edu/sites/default/files/wp2012-030.pdf

Global indicator framework for the Sustainable Development Goals and targets of the 2030 Agenda for Sustainable Development. (n.d.). A/RES/71/313. Retrieved from https://unstats.un.org/sdgs/indicators/Global%20Indicator%20Framework%20after%202022%20refinement_Eng.pdf

Glušac, L. (2017). Protecting the rights of refugees in transit countries: What role for national human rights institutions (NHRIs)? In S. Stanarevic, I. Djordjevic, & V. Rokvic (Eds.), *The Third International Academic Conference on Human Security—Conference Proceedings* (pp. 65–72). University of Belgrade, Faculty of Security Studies.

Glušac, L. (2018a). Local public libraries as human rights intermediaries. *Netherlands Quarterly of Human Rights, 36*(2), 133–151. DOI: https://doi.org/10.1177/0924051918772968

Glušac, L. (2018b). National human rights institutions and oversight of the security services. *Journal of Human Rights Practice, 10*(1), 58–82. DOI: https://doi.org/10.1093/jhuman/huy002

Glušac, L. (2018c). The impact of constitutionalization of ombudsman institutions on their functioning in transitional countries. In B. Djordjević (Ed.), *Constitutionalism and Constitutional Design in Democratic Recession* (pp. 311–326). Proceedings of the 2018 Serbian Political Science Association Annual Conference, Belgrade. (In Serbian)

Glušac, L. (2019a). Assessing the relationship between parliament and ombudsman: Evidence from Serbia (2007–2016). *The International Journal of Human Rights, 23*(4), 531–554, DOI: https://doi.org/10.1080/13642987.2018.1513400

Glušac, L. (2019b). Engagement and political institutions: The case of Ombudsman. *Philosophy and Society, 30*(4), 493–508. DOI: https://doi.org/10.2298/FID1904493G

Glušac, L. (2019c). *The Ombudsman: Models, powers and accountability.* London: Westminster Foundation for Democracy.

Glušac, L. (2019d). The role of national human rights institutions in post-legislative scrutiny. *European Journal of Law Reform, 2,* 72–86.

Glušac, L. (2020). *Strengthening ombudspersons in Central and Eastern Europe*. (Policy Paper No. 7). Berlin: German Marshall Fund of the United States. Retrieved from https://www.gmfus .org/sites/default/files/Glusac%2520-%2520CEE%2520Ombudspersons%2520-%25 2011%2520Jun%2520%2528002%2529.pdf

Glušac, L., & Kuduzovic, A. (2021). Impact of COVID-19 on ombuds institutions for the armed forces (Briefing Note). Geneva: DCAF. Retrieved from https://www.dcaf.ch/sites/default/files /publications/documents/COVID-9_and_OmbudsInstitutions.pdf

Glušac, L. (2021). A critical appraisal of the Venice Principles on the protection and promotion of the Ombudsman: An equivalent to the Paris Principles?. *Human Rights Law Review, 21*(1), 22–53. DOI: https://doi.org/10.1093/hrlr/ngaa040

Glušac, L. (2022). Universal periodic review and policy change: The case of national human rights institutions. *Journal of Human Rights Practice, 14*(1), 285–304. DOI: https://doi.org/10.1093 /jhuman/huab055

Goodman, R., & Pegram, T. (Eds.). (2012). Human rights, state compliance, and social change: Assessing national human rights institutions. Cambridge: Cambridge University Press.

Gordon, E. (2014). Security sector reform, statebuilding and local ownership: Securing the state or its people? *Journal of Intervention and Statebuilding, 8*(2–3), 126–148. DOI: https://doi.org /10.1080/17502977.2014.930219

Graham, J., Amos, B., & Plumptre, T. (2003). *Principles for good governance in the 21st century* (Policy brief No. 15). Institute on Governance. Retrieved from https://pdf4pro.com/cdn/prin ciples-for-policy-brief-in-the-21-good-governance-st-348699.pdf

Grimes, M. (2013). The contingencies of societal accountability: Examining the link between civil society and good government. *Studies in Comparative International Development, 48*(4), 380–402. DOI: https://doi.org/10.1007/s12116-012-9126-3

Grindle, M. (2004). Good enough governance: Poverty reduction and reform in developing countries. *Governance: An International Journal of Policy, Administration, and Institutions, 17*(4), 525–548. DOI: https://doi.org/10.1111/j.0952-1895.2004.00256.x

Hadler, D. (2018, June 30). Heute hilft zum 500. Mal der Bürgeranwalt. *Kleine Zeitung*. Retrieved from https://www.kleinezeitung.at/kultur/medien/5456357/

Hänggi, H. (2004). Conceptualizing security sector reform and reconstruction. In A. Bryden & H. Hänggi (Eds.), Reform and reconstruction of the security sector (pp. 3–20) Berlin: Lit Verlag.

Hanretty, C., & Koop, C. (2013). Shall the law set them free? The formal and actual independence of regulatory agencies. *Regulation & Governance, 7*(2), 195–214. DOI: https://doi.org/10.1111 /j.1748-5991.2012.01156.x

Hins, W., & Voorhoof, D. (2007). Access to state-held information as a fundamental right under the European Convention on Human Rights. *European Constitutional Law Review, 3*(1), 114–126. DOI: https://doi.org/10.1017/S1574019607001149

Holmberg, S., Rothstein, B., & Nasiritousi, N. (2009). Quality of government: What you get. *Annual Review of Political Science, 12*, 135–61. DOI: https://doi.org/10.1146/annurev-polisci -100608-104510

Hyden, G., Court, J., & Mease, K. (2004). Making sense of governance: Empirical evidence from 16 developing countries. Boulder, CO: Lynne Rienner.

International Conference of Ombuds Institutions for the Armed Forces (ICOAF). (2021, October 18–22). 13th ICOAF Conference Statement. Canberra. https://www.13icoaf.org/_files/ugd /b86d90_e7d3603143b34f67a02b0fab042007c5.pdf

International Conference of Ombuds Institutions for the Armed Forces (ICOAF). (2016, October 2–5). 8th ICOAF Conference Statement, Amsterdam. https://www.icoaf.org/_files/ugd/b86d90 _34a2cbc4cc224c9e8c71f76eeb4f97e1.pdf

International Ombudsman Institute (IOI). (2023). *Board members*. Retrieved from https://www
.theioi.org/downloads/6srhc/ioi-board-organizational-chart-en_20230601.pdf

International Telecommunication Union (ITU). (2021, November 30). *2.9 billion people still offline*.
Retrieved from https://www.itu.int/en/mediacentre/Pages/PR-2021-11-29-FactsFigures.aspx

International Telecommunication Union (ITU). (n.d.). *Statistics*. Retrieved from https://www.itu
.int/en/ITU-D/Statistics/Pages/stat/default.aspx

Inter-Parliamentary Union (IPU) and DCAF. (2003). *Parliamentary oversight of the security sector:
Principles, mechanisms and practices*. Geneva: IPU and DCAF.

Jacoby, D. (1999). The future of the ombudsman. In L. C. Reif (Ed.), *The International Ombudsman Anthology*. The Hague-London-Boston: Kluwer Law International.

Janković, S. (2006). Democratic civil control of intelligence: Security services in Serbia. Belgrade:
Belgrade Centre for Security Policy. (In Serbian.)

Jenkins-Smith, H. C., & Herron, K. G. (2009). Rock and a hard place: Public willingness to trade
civil rights and liberties for greater security. *Politics & Policy 37*(5), 1095–1123. DOI: https://
doi.org/10.1111/j.1747-1346.2009.00215.x

Joshi, D. K., & Thimothy, R. (2019). Long-term impacts of parliamentary gender quotas in a sin-
gle-party system: Symbolic co-option or delayed integration?. *International Political Science
Review, 40*(4), 591–606. DOI: https://doi.org/10.1177/0192512118772852

Kagiaros, D. (2015). Protecting 'national security' whistleblowers in the Council of Europe: An
evaluation of three approaches on how to balance national security with freedom of expres-
sion. *The International Journal of Human Rights, 19*(4), 408–484. DOI: https://doi.org/10.1080
/13642987.2015.1027061

Karlsson-Vinkhuyzen S. I., Groff M., Tamás, P. A., Dahl, A. L., Harder, M., & Hassall, G. (2018).
Entry into force and then? The Paris Agreement and state accountability. *Climate Policy, 18*(5),
593–599.

Karlsson-Vinkhuyzen, S., Dahl, A. L., & Persson, Å. (2018). The emerging accountability
regimes for the Sustainable Development Goals and policy integration: Friend or foe?
Environment and Planning C: Politics and Space, 36(8), 1371–1390. DOI: https://doi.org
/10.1177/2399654418779995

Kaufmann, D., Kraay, A., & Zoido-Lobatón, P. (1999). *Governance matters* (World Bank Policy
Research Working Paper 2196). Retrieved from https://elibrary.worldbank.org/doi/epdf
/10.1596/1813-9450-2196

Keefer, P. (2009). Governance. In T. Landman & N. Robinson (Eds.), *The Sage handbook of comparative politics* (pp. 439–462). London: Sage.

Keping, Y. (2018). Governance and good governance: A new framework for political analysis.
Fudan Journal of the Humanities and Social Sciences, 11, 1–8. DOI: https://doi.org/10.1007
/s40647-017-0197-4

Khagram, S., Clark, W., & Firas Raad, D. (2003). From the environment and human security to
sustainable security and development. *Journal of Human Development, 4*(2), 289–313. DOI:
https://doi.org/10.1080/1464988032000087604

Khaitan, T. (2021). Guarantor institutions. *Asian Journal of Comparative Law 16*(S1), S40–S59.
DOI: https://doi.org/10.1017/asjcl.2021.19

Kinzelbach, K., and E. Cole (Eds.). (2007). *Monitoring and investigating the security sector: Recommendations for ombudsman institutions to promote and protect human rights for public security*.
Geneva: UNDP and DCAF.

König-Reis, S. (n.d.). *The role of national human rights institutions and advancing SDG 16
(Module 9). Mainstreaming SDG 16 training course*. Retrieved from https://mainstreamings
dg16.org/table-of-contents/9-the-role-of-national-human-rights-institutions-and-advancing
-sdg-16-produced-by-saionara-konig-reis-danish-institute-for-human-rights/

Kovatch, B. (2016). Sexual exploitation and abuse in UN peacekeeping missions: A case study of MONUC and MONUSCO. *The Journal of the Middle East and Africa, 7*(2), 157–174. DOI: https://doi.org/10.1080/21520844.2016.1192978

Krogstad, E. (2013). *Abundant in policy, absent in practice? Rethinking 'local ownership'* (Chr. Michelsen Institute Working Paper 2013:1). Bergen: Chr. Michelsen Institute.

Kucsko-Stadlmayer, G. (2008). European ombudsman-institutions: A comparative legal analysis regarding the multifaceted realisation of an idea. Vienna: Springer.

Kurtz, M., & Schrank, A. (2007a). Growth and governance: Models, measures, and mechanisms. *The Journal of Politics, 69*(2), 538–554. DOI: https://doi.org/10.1111/j.1468-2508.2007.00549.x

Kurtz, M., & Schrank, A. (2007b). Growth and governance: A defense. *The Journal of Politics, 69*(2), 563–569. DOI: https://doi.org/10.1111/j.1468-2508.2007.00551.x

Laberge, M., & Touihri, N. (2019). Can SDG 16 data drive national accountability? A cautiously optimistic view. *Global Policy, 10*(S1), S153–S156.

Lacatus, C., & Carraro, V. (20230.) National human rights institutions: Independent actors in global human rights governance?. *International Affairs, 99*(3), 1167–1189. DOI: https://doi.org/10.1093/ia/iiad077

Langtry, D., & Roberts Lyer, K. (2021). National human rights institutions: Rules, requirements and practice. Oxford: Oxford University Press.

Law on the Protector of Citizens. (2021). *Official gazette of the Republic of Serbia*, No.105/2021.

Lee, S., & Bartels, S. (2020). 'They put a few coins in your hand to drop a baby in you': A study of peacekeeper-fathered children in Haiti. *International Peacekeeping, 27*(2), 177–209. DOI: https://doi.org/10.1080/13533312.2019.1698297

Lockwood, M. (2010). Good governance for terrestrial protected areas: A framework, principles and performance outcomes. *Journal of Environmental Management, 91*(3), 754–766. DOI: https://doi.org/10.1016/j.jenvman.2009.10.005

Lührmann, A., Marquardt, K. L., & Mechkova, V. (2020). Constraining governments: New indices of vertical, horizontal, and diagonal accountability. *American Political Science Review, 114*(3), 811–820. DOI: https://doi.org/10.1017/S0003055420000222

Lyon, D. (2010). National IDs in a global world: Surveillance, security and citizenship. *Case Western Reserve Journal of International Law, 42*(3), 607–623.

MacNaughton, G. (2017). Vertical inequalities: Are the SDGs and human rights up to the challenges?. *The International Journal of Human Rights, 21*(8), 1050–1072. DOI: https://doi.org/10.1080/13642987.2017.1348697

Mæhlum, M. (2008). Human rights monitoring. In S. Skåre, I. Burkey & H. Mørk (Eds.), *Manual on human rights monitoring. An introduction for human rights field officers* (pp. 1–26). Oslo: Norwegian Centre for Human Rights.

Martin, A., & Wilson, P. (2008). Security sector evolution: Which locals? Ownership of what? In T. Donais (Ed.), *Local ownership and security sector reform* (pp. 83–103). Geneva: DCAF.

McDermott, W. (2021). Ombuds institutions for the armed forces. In DCAF and ODIHR, *Human rights of armed forces personnel: Compendium of standards, good practices and recommendations* (pp. 327–351), Geneva and Warsaw: DCAF and OSCE/ODIHR.

McGregor, L., Murray, R., & Shipman, S. (2019). Should national human rights institutions institutionalize dispute resolution? *Human Rights Quarterly, 41*(2), 309–339. DOI: https://doi.org/10.1353/hrq.2019.0028

Mcinerney-Lankford, S. (2009). Human rights and development: A comment on challenges and opportunities from a legal perspective. *Journal of Human Rights Practice, 1*(1), 51–82. DOI: https://doi.org/10.1093/jhuman/hun005

McMillan, J. (2004, November). *The ombudsman and the rule of law* (speech addressed during the Public Law Weekend, Canberra). Retrieved from www.ombudsman.gov.au/speeches-and-presentations/

Mérida Declaration. (2015). *The Mérida Declaration: The role of national human rights institutions in implementing the 2030 Agenda for Sustainable Development.* https://nhri.ohchr.org/EN/ICC/InternationalConference/12IC/Background%20Information/Merida%20Declaration%20FINAL.pdf

Merry, S. E. (2011). Measuring the world: Indicators, human rights, and global governance. *Current Anthropology 52* (Supplement 3), S83–S95. DOI: https://doi.org/10.1086/657241

Meuleman, L. (2019, May 1). What makes effective governance? Retrieved from https://www.un.org/development/desa/undesavoice/more-from-undesa/2019/05/44903.html

Mitrović, Lj., & Romić, V. (2017). The role of the media in discharge of function of the Ombudsman/The Protector of the Rights of Citizens. In I. Stevanović & O. Pavićević (Eds.), *Judiciary and media* (pp. 89–100). Belgrade: Institute of Criminological and Sociological Research Belgrade.

Mobekk, E. (2010). Security sector reform and the challenges of ownership. In M. Sedra (Ed.), *The future of security sector reform* (pp. 230–243). Waterloo: CIGI.

Myrttinen, H. (2019). Security sector governance, security sector reform and gender. In *Gender and Security Toolkit No. 1. Geneva: DCAF, OSCE/ODIHR and UN Women.* Retrieved from https://www.dcaf.ch/sites/default/files/publications/documents/GSToolkit_Tool-1%20EN%20FINAL_2.pdf

Nathan, L. (2008). The challenge of local ownership of SSR: From donor rhetoric to practice. In T. Donais (Ed.), *Local ownership and security sector reform* (pp. 19–38). Geneva: DCAF.

Neave, C. (2014, November 28). *Exploring the role of the Commonwealth Ombudsman in relation to Parliament* (Senate Occasional Lecture Series at Parliament House), Canberra. Retrieved from https://www.aph.gov.au/About_Parliament/Senate/Whats_On/Seminars_and_Lectures///link.aspx?_id¼E60F46 B05BBA40699E152F1D06A17834&_z¼z

Nordås, R., & Rustad, S. C. A. (2013). Sexual exploitation and abuse by peacekeepers: Understanding variation. *International Interactions, 39*(4), 511–534. DOI: https://doi.org/10.1080/03050629.2013.805128

O'Donnell, G. A. (1998). Horizontal accountability in new democracies. *Journal of Democracy, 9*(3), 112–126.

OHCHR. (n.d.). *About good governance.* Retrieved from https://www.ohchr.org/en/good-governance/about-good-governance

OHCHR. (2001). *Training manual on human rights monitoring.* New York: United Nations. Retrieved from https://www.ohchr.org/sites/default/files/Documents/Publications/training7Introen.pdf

OHCHR. (2007). *Good governance practices for the protection of human rights.* New York and Geneva: United Nations. Retrieved from https://www.ohchr.org/sites/default/files/Documents/Publications/GoodGovernance.pdf

OHCHR. (2010). *National human rights institutions: History, principles, roles and responsibilities* (Professional Training Series No. 4). Geneva: OHCHR.

OHCHR. (2012). *Strengthening the bond between parliaments and national human rights institutions.* Retrieved from http://www.ohchr.org/EN/NewsEvents/Pages/ParliamentsAndNHRIs.aspx#sthash.0Skc8vHg.dpuf

Oosterveld, W., & Galand, R. (2012). Justice reform, security sector reform and local ownership. *Hague Journal on the Rule of Law, 4*(1), 194–209. DOI: https://doi.org/10.1017/S1876404512000115

Organisation for Economic Co-operation and Development (OECD). (2007). *The OECD DAC handbook on security system reform (SSR): Supporting security and justice.* Paris: OECD.

Organisation for Economic Cooperation and Development (OECD). (2020). *States of fragility.* Retrieved from https://www.oecd-ilibrary.org/sites/ba7c22e7-en/1/2/5/index.html?itemId=/content/publication/ba7c22e7-en&_csp_=89578a182071559ff79c670c40753038&itemIGO=oecd&itemContentType=book

Owen, S. (1993). The ombudsman: Essential elements and common challenges. In L. C. Reif, M. A. Marshall & C. Ferris (Eds.), *The Ombudsman: Diversity and development.* (pp. 1–17) Edmonton: International Ombudsman Institute.

Parliamentary Assembly of the Council of Europe (PACE). (2010, April 29). Resolution 1729 (2010) on the Protection of Whistleblowers.

Pearman, V. (2020, November). *COVID-19 and the Ombudsperson – Rising to the challenge of a pandemic* (speech delivered at international webinar organized by the State Comptroller and Ombudsman of Israel, under the auspices of the IOI). Retrieved from https://www.theioi.org/ioi-news /current-news/re-watch-our-webinar-on-covid-19-with-contributions-from-around-theglobe

Peruzzotti, E., & Smulovitz C. (Eds.). (2006). Enforcing the rule of law: Social accountability in the new Latin American democracies. Pittsburgh: University of Pittsburgh Press.

Petrović, P., & Pejić Nikić, J. (Eds.). (2020). *Security sector capture in Serbia: An early study.* Belgrade, Belgrade Centre for Security Policy.

Pinheiro, P. S. (2006). *World report on violence against children.* Report of the independent expert for the United Nations study on violence against children.

Pogge, T., & Sengupta, M. (2016). Assessing the sustainable development goals from a human rights perspective. *Journal of International and Comparative Social Policy, 32*(2), 83–97. DOI: https://doi.org/10.1080/21699763.2016.1198268

Pomeranz, E. F., & Stedman, R. C. (2020). Measuring good governance: Piloting an instrument for evaluating good governance principles. *Journal of Environmental Policy & Planning, 22*(3), 428–440. DOI: https://doi.org/10.1080/1523908X.2020.1753181

Putnam, R., with Leonardi, R., & Nanetti, R. (1993). Making democracy work: Civic traditions in modern Italy. Princeton: Princeton University Press.

Qehaja, F., & Prezelj, I. (2017). Issues of local ownership in Kosovo's security sector, *Southeast European and Black Sea Studies, 17*(3), 403–419. DOI: https://doi.org/10.1080/14683857.2017 .1324279

Reif, L. C. (2004). The ombudsman, good governance and the international human rights system. Leiden-Boston: Martinus Nijhoff.

Remac, M. (2014). Coordinating ombudsmen and the judiciary. Cambridge: Intersentia.

Roosevelt, E. (1958). *The great question* (speech delivered at the United Nations on March 27, 1958).

Rose-Ackerman, S. (1996). Democracy and 'grand' corruption. *International Social Science Journal 48*(149), 365–380.

Sachs, J. D. (2012). From millennium development goals to sustainable development goals. *Lancet, 379*, 2206–2211.

Satterthwaite, M. L., & Dhital S. (2019). *Measuring access to justice: Transformation and technicality in SDG 16.3.* Global Policy, 10 (Supplement 1), S96–S109. DOI: https://doi.org/10.1111 /1758-5899.12597

Scheye, E., & Peake, G. (2005). Unknotting local ownership. In A. Ebnother & P. Fluri (Eds.), *After intervention: Public security in post-conflict societies—From intervention to sustainable local ownership* (pp. 235–260). Geneva: DCAF/PfP Consortium of Defence Academies and Security Studies Institutes.

Schnabel, A. (2012). The security-development discourse and the role of SSR as a development instrument. In A. Schnabel & V. Farr (Eds.), Back to the roots: Security sector reform and development (pp. 29–76). Münster: LIT Verlag.

SDG Tracker. (n.d. A). *Developing country participation in international organizations.* Retrieved from https://sdg-tracker.org/peace-justice

SDG Tracker. (n.d. B). *Promote just, peaceful and inclusive societies.* Retrieved from https://sdg -tracker.org/peace-justice

Sengupta, A. (2001). *Third report of the independent expert on the right to development*, submitted in accordance with Commission resolution 2000/5. Retrieved from https://digitallibrary.un.org/record/431577#record-files-collapse-header.

Shinoda, H. (2008). The difficulty and importance of local ownership and capacity development in peacebuilding. *Hiroshima Peace Science 30*, 95–115. DOI: https://doi.org/10.15027/30968

Skogly, S. (2001). The human rights obligations of the World Bank and the International Monetary Fund. London: Cavendish Press.

Sperfeldt, C. (2021). Legal identity in the sustainable development agenda: Actors, perspectives and trends in an emerging field of research. *The International Journal of Human Rights, 22*(6), 217–238. DOI: https://doi.org/10.1080/13642987.2021.1913409

Spigelman, J. (2004). The integrity branch of government. *Australian Law Journal, 78*(11), 724.

Stern M., & Öjendal J. (2010). Mapping the security–development nexus: Conflict, complexity, cacophony, convergence? *Security Dialogue, 41*(1), 5–29. DOI: https://doi.org/10.1177/0967010609357041

Tatarenko, A. (n.d.). *12 principles of good governance*. Retrieved from https://www.bpe.al/en/12-principles-good-governance

Teshome, R. G. (2022). The draft convention on the right to development: A new dawn to the recognition of the right to development as a human right? *Human Rights Law Review, 22*(2). DOI: https://doi.org/10.1093/hrlr/ngac001

The 2030 Agenda. (2015). *Transforming our world: The 2030 Agenda for sustainable development*. Retrieved from https://sdgs.un.org/2030agenda

The Protector of Citizens of the Republic of Serbia. (2011). *2010 annual report*. Retrieved from https://www.ombudsman.org.rs/attachments/052_Annual%20Report%202010.pdf

The Protector of Citizens of the Republic of Serbia. (2012). *The report on the 'legally invisible' people in the Republic of Serbia* (in Serbian). Retrieved from https://www.pravamanjina.rs/attachments/Izvestaj%20o%20polozaju%20Pravno%20Nevidljivih%20Lica%20u%20RS.pdf

The Protector of Citizens of the Republic of Serbia. (2013). 2012 annual report. Retrieved from https://www.ombudsman.org.rs/attachments/052_Annual%20Report%202012.pdf

The Protector of Citizens of the Republic of Serbia. (2021). Child protection policy. Retrieved from https://www.pravadeteta.com/attachments/article/1057/Child%20Protection%20Policy.pdf

TST. (n.d.). TST Issues Brief: *Means of implementation; Global partnership for achieving sustainable development*. Retrieved from https://sustainablevdevelopment.un.org/content/documents/2079Issues%20Brief%20Means%20of%20Implementation%20Final_TST_141013.pdf

Tushnet, M. (2021). The new fourth branch: Institutions for protecting constitutional democracy. Cambridge: Cambridge University Press. DOI: https://doi.org/10.1017/9781009047609

Twomey, P. (2007). Human rights-based approaches to development: Towards accountability. In M. A. Baderin, & R. McCorquodale (Eds.), *Economic, social and cultural rights in action* (pp. 45–69). Oxford: Oxford University Press.

UK Law Commission (UK Law Com). (2006). *Post-legislative scrutiny* (Report No. 302).

UN Broadband Commission for Sustainable Development. (2017). *The state of broadband*. Retrieved from https://www.itu.int/dms_pub/itu-s/opb/pol/S-POL-BROADBAND.18-2017-PDF-E.pdf

UN Economic and Social Council (Un ECOSOC). (2018). *Principles of effective governance for sustainable development*, E/2018/44-E/C.16/2018/8, Retrieved from https://publicadministration.un.org/Portals/1/Images/CEPA/Principles_of_effective_governance_english.pdf

UN General Assembly (UNGA). (1993). *Resolution 48/134 Principles relating to the Status of National Institutions (The Paris Principles)*.

UN General Assembly (UNGA). (2012). *Report of the Secretary General: National institutions for the promotion and protection of human rights. Annex: Belgrade Principles on the relationship between NHRIs and parliaments*, A/HRC/20/9.

UNDP. (1997). *Governance for sustainable human development, An integrated paper on the highlights of four regional consultation workshops on governance for sustainable human development.* Retrieved from https://digitallibrary.un.org/record/3831662

UNDP. (2011). *Governance principles, institutional capacity and quality.* Retrieved from https://www.undp.org/content/dam/undp/library/Poverty%20Reduction/Inclusive%20development/Towards%20Human%20Resilience/Towards_SustainingMDGProgress_Ch8.pdf

UNDP. (2017). Monitoring to implement peaceful, just and inclusive societies–Pilot initiative on national-level monitoring of SDG 16. New York: UNDP.

UNDP. (2018). *What does it mean to leave no one behind?* (A UNDP discussion paper and framework for implementation). New York: United Nations. Retrieved from https://www.undp.org/sites/g/files/zskgke326/files/publications/Discussion_Paper_LNOB_EN_lres.pdf

UNICEF. (2020). *NHRIs and monitoring children's rights in closed settings.* Retrieved from https://www.unicef.org/eca/media/15326/file

United Nations (1998, August 27). *Annual Report of the Secretary-General on the work of the organization.* Retrieved from http://www.un.org/Docs/SG/Report98/ch2.htm

United Nations. (2012). *Security sector reform: Integrated technical guidance notes, UN Inter-Agency Security Sector Reform Task Force (IASSRTF).* Retrieved from https://securitysectorintegrity.com/publication/security-sector-reform-integrated-technical-guidance-notes

United Nations (UN). (2022). *Progress towards the Sustainable Development Goals, Report of the Secretary-General.* Retrieved from https://sustainabledevelopment.un.org/content/documents/29858SG_SDG_Progress_Report_2022.pdf

United Nations Department of Peacekeeping Operations (UN DPKO) (2012). *The United Nations SSR perspective. Office of rule of law and security institutions.* New York: United Nations. Retrieved from https://peacekeeping.un.org/sites/default/files/ssr_perspective_2012.pdf

United Nations Legal Identity Expert Group. (2019). *United Nations strategy for legal identity for all (Concept Note).* Retrieved from https://unstats.un.org/legal-identity-agenda/documents/UN-Strategy-for-LIA.pdf

United Nations. (2004). A more secure world: Our shared responsibility, report of the Secretary-General's high-level panel on threats, challenges and change. New York: United Nations.

United Nations. (2012). *Security sector reform: Integrated technical guidance notes. UN Inter-Agency Security Sector Reform Task Force (IASSRTF).* Retrieved from https://securitysectorintegrity.com/publication/security-sector-reform-integrated-technical-guidance-notes

UN SDG. (2003). *The human rights based approach to development cooperation towards a common understanding among UN agencies.* Retrieved from https://unsdg.un.org/resources/human-rights-based-approach-development-cooperation-towards-common-understanding-among-un

UN Stats. (2021, April 1). *SDG indicator metadata.* Retrieved from https://unstats.un.org/sdgs/metadata/files/Metadata-16-03-03.pdf

UN Stats. (n.d.). *Note on developed and developing regions.* Retrieved from https://unstats.un.org/unsd/methodology/m49/

Venice Commission (2019). *Principles on the protection and promotion of the ombudsman institution ('The Venice Principles').* Retrieved from https://www.venice.coe.int/webforms/documents/default.aspx?pdffile=CDL-AD(2019)005-e

Vladisavljević, N., Krstić, A., & Pavlovic, J. (2019). Communicating power and resistance in democratic decline: The 2015 smear campaign against Serbia's Ombudsman. In K. Voltmer et al (Eds.), *Media, communication and the struggle for democratic change: Case studies on contested transitions* (pp. 205–228). Cham: Palgrave Macmillan.

Weiss, T. (2000). Governance, good governance and global governance: Conceptual and actual challenges. *Third World Quarterly, 21*(5), 795–814.

Whistleblowing International Network. (2019, June 7). *Voice and dissent in the military.* Retrieved from https://whistleblowingnetwork.org/Our-Work/Spotlight/Stories/test-5

Winkler, I. T., & Satterthwaite, M. L. (2017). Leaving no one behind? Persistent inequalities in the SDGs. *The International Journal of Human Rights, 21*(8), 1073–1097. DOI: https://doi.org/10.1080/13642987.2017.1348702

World Bank. (2016). *By the numbers: The cost of war & peace in the Middle East.* Retrieved from http://www.worldbank.org/en/news/feature/2016/02/03/by-the-numbers-the-cost-of-war-and-peace-in-mena

World Health Organization (WHO). (2002). *World report on violence and health: Summary.* Geneva: WHO: Retrieved from https://www.who.int/violence_injury_prevention/violence/world_report/en/summary_en.pdf

Wouters, J., & Meuwissen, K. (Eds.). (2013). National human rights institutions in Europe: Comparative, European and international perspectives. Cambridge: Intersentia.

Zeid Ra'ad Al Hussein. (2015, September 25). *An agenda for equality* (Statement of the United Nations High Commissioner for Human Rights at the Summit for Adoption of the Post-2015 Development Agenda, UN Headquarters, New York). Retrieved from https://www.ohchr.org/en/2015/09/statement-zeid-raad-al-hussein-united-nations-high-commissioner-human-rights-summit

www.ingramcontent.com/pod-product-compliance
Lightning Source LLC
Chambersburg PA
CBHW061218270326
41926CB00028B/4683